Iterate or Die:
Agile Consulting for 21st Century Business Success

Eric Berridge

Michael Kirven

With a foreword by Marc Benioff

authorHOUSE®

AuthorHouse™
1663 Liberty Drive, Suite 200
Bloomington, IN 47403
www.authorhouse.com
Phone: 1-800-839-8640

First published by AuthorHouse 9/02/2008

Interior layout/graph illustrations by April Mostek.
Cover design by April Mostek.
Content assistance by Alan Radding.

ISBN: 978-1-4389-1224-0 (sc)
ISBN: 978-1-4389-1223-3 (dj)

Printed in the United States of America
Bloomington, Indiana

This book is printed on acid-free paper.

Library of Congress Control Number: 2008907888

Contents

Foreword
by Marc Benioff

When we founded salesforce.com in 1999, we had a simple idea: build business applications that were as easy to use as eBay or Amazon.com. Under the hood was a powerful enterprise-class relational database that we offered as a service to customers of all sizes. No software to buy, no hardware to set up. Software as a service was born, and customers discovered the power and convenience of cloud computing.

The rise of salesforce.com and SaaS raised profound questions for the IT consulting business. There was no longer a need for a firm to install, patch, test, performance test, and troubleshoot complex software, hardware, and storage. These tasks have traditionally represented 50-70% of most IT consulting engagements. Naturally, some traditional players balked at the idea of SaaS and IT consultants as partners.

The disruptive force of salesforce.com and SaaS created an opportunity for a new breed of consulting, and an increased focus on customer success has been the direct result. Consulting 2.0, if you will, has a few key tenets:

1) Focus on success criteria instead of functionality.
2) Focus on client self-sufficiency.
3) Focus on change management.

Now there is an impressive list of thousands of successful SaaS engagements with this new class of visionary consultants that have embraced the opportunity to define a new standard of excellence for customer success.

Behind these key principles is some radical rethinking of the change process itself.

One key principal inherent in Consulting 2.0 is the idea of agile software development. Agile deployment methodologies rely on quick, 30 day deliverables, as opposed to the lengthier time-frames associated with traditional waterfall methodologies. In witnessing the rise of Consulting

2.0, we are also witnessing the rise and success of these new agile methodologies. Companies like salesforce.com <http://salesforce.com/>, eBay, Google, and Bluewolf all rely on agile development to make cloud computing transparent, productive, and successful.

Acknowledgements

Above and beyond anyone else, we would like to thank
the clients that have embraced the ideas in this book,
helping us to refine
the optimal approach to 21st century consulting.

Eric Berridge and Michael Kirven
April 2008

1

It's a New Consulting World Out There

It seems almost quaint now, but less than 20 years ago, scientists and the media were dreaming big about the nascent Internet, and its astounding potential as a so-called "Information Superhighway." Futuristic predictions rarely bear out as imagined, but in the case of the Internet, the projections were surprisingly accurate. If anything, we underestimated the sweeping social changes widespread Internet use would herald, back when we were still dabbling with its early iterations in academic and industry settings. The technological advances that supported the development and exponential growth of the World Wide Web and catapulted the Internet into homes, along with the rapid, global embrace of this groundbreaking communication network, paved the way for unprecedented business experiments.

Enthusiasm for this burgeoning communication technology spurred a rush to the Internet, with businesses of all sizes eager to establish a web presence. Pizza shops built websites, retailers posted their catalogs online, and large enterprises launched entirely new web-based business units. Opportunities for business innovation and growth seemed endless—never before had technology allowed instantaneous, simultaneous information, image, and sound transfer, *and* an opportunity to interface with millions of customers, all who could essentially customize their experience while online. Pundits heralded a new economy, one that seemed remarkably removed from such old-fashioned notions as actual revenue or, even profit. Venture capitalists, eager to stake their bets on Internet enterprises, fueled the dotcom boom, seeding countless startups with millions of dollars in capital. With each IPO, stock prices for the dotcoms reached new heights, encouraging ever-greater investment in these new ventures.

What is surprising in retrospect is the extent to which established business models were collectively ignored or abandoned in the face of this new technology. Perhaps executives and venture capitalists were blinded by its dazzle. Some may have believed that old business rules wouldn't apply in a new media. That may be what ultimately doomed so many dotcoms. Startups with bloated budgets blew millions on marketing—consider the Pets.com sock puppet gracing the airwaves during the Superbowl. But the notion that page views would necessarily translate to revenue was a flimsy one. When the internet bubble burst after two heady years of ballooning stock prices, businesses and investors were left with the hard-learned lesson that even on the web, solid business practices were essential for a company to survive and thrive. Of course, in the mid-1990's, just as mania for the Internet was beginning to brew, the only doomsday scenarios anyone foresaw were related to the Millennium Bug. Consultants, who were already in demand on Internet-related projects, were now called in to address the Y2K problem. Often, they'd install new Y2K-compliant Enterprise Resource Planning systems (ERPs), which were being touted as a panacea for multiple system-related ills, such as non-integrated or unsynchronized data. Sold on the value of ERP, or big enterprise integrated software applications meant to support Customer Relationship Management (CRM), executives proudly declared that—beyond assuring Y2K compliance—their new systems would streamline core business processes and automatically align the business with proven industry best practices.

The companies that may have benefited most were the enterprise software vendors and consulting firms, including Oracle, SAP, Peoplesoft,

IBM, Siebel Systems, Anderson Consulting, KPMG, Deloitte and Touche, and Price Waterhouse. Consulting firms in particular were recruiting and expanding at an unprecedented rate. New ones joined the mix. Companies like Scient, Viant, IXL, USWeb, and Sapient attracted Ivy Leaguers and MBAs who'd begun to shun finance and real estate in favor of IT jobs.

Whether we successfully mitigated disaster, or whether the Y2K scenarios were simply overblown remains debatable. Regardless, planes didn't fall from the sky, banking systems didn't fail, factories didn't grind to a halt, utilities didn't go dark, and hospital operating rooms continued to function. In the meantime, the new rules-defying Internet enterprises and the much-hyped ERP systems weren't faring as well. Dotcom start-ups were hemorrhaging money, while companies that had championed the use of enterprise resource software now found themselves stuck with what was essentially shelfware.

Despite huge investments in these software systems, in practice they were barely, rarely, or never used for productive work. A few employees might manage to use a few pieces of it, but generally, companies found program installation, use, or modification too difficult. Systems were often irrelevant before the implementation and training were complete. Companies that hoped to salvage use of these systems also turned to consultants. Because they were so in-demand, IT consultants commanded incredible rates for their Internet expertise and Y2K troubleshooting. Two-year, eight-figure ERP implementations were common; three-year, nine-figure ERP implementations were not unheard of. Yet some firms had no compunction about dispatching large teams of inexperienced consultants to implement complex ERP systems. Or, multiple teams top-heavy with consultants were involved in a single project.

Practices like these may have been good for consulting firms' bottom lines, but they were decidedly bad for their clients. Company executives who hired these consultants shared the blame for poor business decisions. In their enthusiasm for high profile projects, executives forgot about results, about defining what they wanted to achieve from these projects, and about how these projects should advance their business objectives. And few consulting firms at that time had interest in helping executives to sort those issues out.

Back in the late 1990's, we worked at InterWorld, a small software company in Manhattan that promised to automate the selling of goods over the Internet. Though InterWorld's technology was impressive, its marketing wasn't, and the company was never heralded as a leading edge operation. We competed in the same space as upstarts such as Broadvision, ATG, and InterShop—all companies that came to market fast, raised immense amounts of capital in both private and public markets, and flamed out as quickly as they had risen to prominence. Ultimately, technology trumped slick marketing, and InterWorld's software earned the company prominent clients, including Disney, Nike, and Toys "R" Us. Ecommerce software vendors, for a brief two-year stretch, were positioned to take over the world, and all of our stock prices—including those of companies such as Ariba and Commerce One—went through the roof.

Those companies that were lucky enough to pull off a secondary offering (InterWorld was not one of them) hung around and milked their cash for as long as possible, but the growth expectations that had supported their lofty valuations were quickly forgotten. There are many lessons to be learned from the ecommerce software crash, but even more telling for us were the lessons to be learned from the software consulting firms that crashed.

US Web—a conglomeration of franchises that perhaps represented the most ridiculous business plan ever—Whitman Hart, Sapient, Razorfish, Inforte, Arthur Anderson Business Consulting, Agency.com. We don't want to denigrate these organizations, but their business models and practices do give some insight into why they failed and, more importantly, the lessons we can apply today to ensure that consulting firms—and IT consultants in general—don't repeat their mistakes. In the pages that follow, we'll explore how firms erred—sometimes fatally—in detail. And we'll look closely at why common practice isn't always the wise choice. For example, as an overarching rule, the IT consulting firms of the 1990s held the project sacred. But dependence on project-basis jobs meant that once a firm landed a client, there was pressure to try to parlay that gig— whether it was the installation of SAP or the construction of a multi-million dollar website—into as long-term an arrangement as possible. Yet as the NASDAQ soared, so did confidence in the new dotcoms. Now, it was the companies that felt dependent on their IT consultants, who in turn, were emboldened to make recommendations that best suited their own business needs. We witnessed these developments firsthand and that gave us an incredible perspective on IT consulting that inspired us to start Bluewolf. Our observations, successes, and lessons learned inspired us to write this book and to share what we've come to consider the best practices in IT consulting.

We'll start with our First Law of Consulting Economics: *Projects don't matter, results matter.* Shareholders don't care about projects; they care about results. Yet prominent companies—perhaps because they've been sold on the importance of projects themselves—have made the mistake of touting them as selling points. I recall seeing a Colgate Palmolive Annual Report from the mid 1990s that linked an SAP project to an earnings shortfall, yet went on to justify the loss by plugging the project as the future of the company. It wasn't, nor was Colgate's future strength determined by the project.

The Second Law of Consulting Economics goes hand in hand with the first. We think of it as the technology fallacy: *A successful business process trumps cool technology.* In other words, business results are more important than an investment in the newest or hottest technology. That means it is often more important—and effective—to automate a company through its culture, with respect for the employees, their training, and their processes, than it is to try to maximize the utility of a particular software application. Throughout this book, we'll elucidate these—and several other hard-learned Laws of Consulting Economics.

Perhaps you are a manager, director, or C-Level executive who hires or has hired consulting firms. We know it's a real possibility that you may have felt slighted or disappointed by consulting firms in the past. Or maybe you are a consultant who is looking for some new ideas about the future of consulting, in which case you may be disappointed in *us* right now for suggesting that working with consultants is sometimes, *well,* disappointing We don't blame you. Consultants generally are honest and hardworking people. The problem is that the conventional business software consulting process and model is broken. In fact, we maintain that it never worked in the first place.

The conventional software consulting process relies on the waterfall model. In its strictest sense, that means progress on the project moves through a series of regimented steps, with one phase flowing into the next as each process is completed. Practically, this may play out with a team of consultants arriving to interview employees, assess the company's processes and systems, and conduct a gap analysis to see where those systems fall short. Just getting to this point can take a large team of consultants months to complete. The result is a requirements specification. Only then will the consultants move on to the design phase—often passing the approved requirements specification off to the coders who will design new processes and systems capable of closing the gaps or troubleshooting identified problems. Eventually, the consultants will present a prototype, which—assuming it is acceptable—will still need to be integrated, tested, installed, and maintained.

For a modern business, the waterfall model—and many of its variations—is destined to fail even before the first interview begins. That's because the process doesn't account for or assess the possibility of changes affecting the business along the way. The rigidity of the waterfall model is an issue, but an even bigger concern is the compartmentalization of the various stages. As each team of consultants sends their discrete stage of the process down the proverbial waterfall, there's a very real chance that they are sending along information that is essentially obsolete. That so much time is invested on the work at each stage only compounds the problem. Successful businesses and the markets they operate in are dynamic. But a consulting firm that employs the waterfall model will lack the flexibility to deliver equally dynamic, responsive software. At best, these firm's prototypes may reflect the state of the business at the time the requirements document was approved. For any client seeking to maintain a competitive edge, that's simply not good enough.

Making changes to the prototype's architecture after delivery isn't a viable solution—it's far too costly, and can take nearly as long as the first-pass development. By the time the finished production system is delivered and implemented, and employees are trained to use it, it may be woefully out of date. So the very consultants who toiled away on custom development of ultimately useless software may resort to recommending off-the-shelf software. And that means those same consultants must return to upgrade a system that was only recently implemented—as if the initial implementation wasn't expensive or disruptive enough.

Viable businesses need top-notch IT support, and they cannot afford to absorb the mistakes or poor judgment of IT consultants. That's why we're writing this book—to tell you that it doesn't have to be this way, that your business can be dynamic and change as often as necessary, and that there is a way for consultants to deliver software that does what you need, when you need it, and can be changed when you need to change it. And we're happy to report that competent service needn't come with an astronomical fee attached.

Leading edge software developers call the highly dynamic, iterative development process we favor *agile development*. It embodies extreme programming with fast deliverables and with clients actively participating in the process every step of the way. At Bluewolf we've applied iterative agile development concepts to business software consulting and combined it with new forms of software delivery to create what amounts to iterative consulting for business agility. Our motto and approach is reflected in our Third Law of Consulting Economics: *Iterate or die*. Businesses that cannot change quickly will not survive in today's highly competitive, highly dynamic markets. You have to be agile, to be able to change, to iterate your business processes; and the software that supports those processes has to change with you. Companies that can't adapt face extinction. Like we say, iterate or die.

With an iterative approach, consultants deliver tangible value that generates real business results in 30 days. That's not to say they will address every function in that time, but that there will be some measurable change that ideally benefits the business. The beauty of this approach is that mistakes are never catastrophic. In fact, they are simply another way to learn about a company's needs. If something doesn't work, it can be modified. Adding functionality is possible. Software can change in response to new competitors, or unanticipated government regulations. The waterfall approach is unforgiving of specification errors, which ultimately amplifies the impact of mistakes or changes. Couple that with the fact that typically, large teams of consultants are necessary to sustain a waterfall-style project, and the cost—both literal and figurative—can skyrocket. With the iterative approach, no more than one month of work—likely done by a couple of consultants—may be "lost"—even if change becomes necessary. And as we've explained, even errors can prove productive with the iterative model.

This book will introduce you to a new approach to software consulting. This isn't a methodology cookbook. To the contrary, it is a framework for a new way to get the systems and functionality you need now and in the future without rigid methodologies. It defines an approach that will let you shape your business in ways that simply have not been possible before. So that the next time consultants carrying three-ring methodology binders stroll into your office with a proposal to "fix" your business, you will know exactly what to say. And, if you've read what follows, it won't be an automatic "yes."

In the following pages we will address:

> The rise and fall of traditional consulting and the difference between consulting and outsourcing;

> The emergence of a new breed of consulting firm;

> The lessons to be gleaned from agile development;

> The development of iterative, agile consulting and the birth of Bluewolf;

> The imperative to empower the customer;

> The software conundrum, the rise of integrated enterprise software packages, and shelfware;

> The people paradox: Who will do the work?

> New vs. old staffing models;

> Liberating customers to focus on their business;

> The rise of Chief Process Officer;

> The new packaged software model;

> The end of HR as we know it: A new staffing model;

> Outsourcing and offshoring;

> The 21st century consultant;

> The Bluewolf Group methodology—agile, iterative consulting;

> The extreme consulting process and model;

> The client experience;

> The new consulting financial model;

> The supporting technologies;
> The critical role of collaboration and communication;
> Driving adoption;
> Agile consulting best practices.

At the end of book you will find a number of useful appendices:

> Laws of Consulting Economics;
> Glossary;
> IT Salary Guide;
> IT Hiring Tips;
> Bluewolf AppExchange modules;
> Sample success plan.

2
The Age of the Dinosaurs

"Modern management consulting had its origins in the 1920s and 1930s," wrote Christopher McKenna in The World's Newest Profession: Management Consulting in the Twentieth Century *(Cambridge University Press, 2006). The following 60 years represented the rise and fall of modern consulting—or what we often think of as the Age of the Dinosaurs—at least for business software consulting.*

Consulting is a broad field, encompassing a wide range of activities and specializations. There's management consulting, dominated by firms like McKinsey & Company, Booz Allen Hamilton and Bain & Company. Heavy hitters in engineering consulting include Bechtel and Halliburton, while IBM Global Services, Accenture, and BearingPoint rank among the IT consulting leaders. Some of the above-mentioned companies consult on outsourcing as well, though offshore firms like Wipro and Infosys are among the most prominent outsourcers. Other niches in the consulting realm range from architecture and design, to facilities management. The focus of this book is on IT consulting, and even more specifically, on business software consulting, or the practice of helping businesses build or acquire, design, implement, customize, and manage software for the purpose of achieving business results. That's what we do; it used to be what all the IT consulting firms did. Some say they still do it; in reality, most have dropped software consulting as a primary part of their practices.

Remember the Big Eight? Use of that term marked the zenith of the American IT consulting firms. Most of the Big Eight were associated with accounting firms. IT consulting was a great extension of the accounting firm, especially since the early big IT systems were transaction processing systems integrally linked with the accounting and financial systems. These were the very systems that morphed into ERP and other integrated enterprise systems—the ones that frequently became shelfware.

The traditional consulting process couldn't have been slower, more costly, and more likely to deliver outdated results if it had been designed expressly for that purpose. Yet it seems no one questioned or proposed alternatives to a process that essentially boiled down to this: consultants attempted to learn all they could about a business by interviewing its top executives, then said, "I will think about this, and show you how to do it better." In response to whatever business ills had been identified, the consultants typically recommended new software and systems, which they would design and build. Of course, the same consultants would help deploy and maintain that system. The process could take months or years, and the client incurred fees at every stage from fact finding and design, through implementation, training, and maintenance.

If fluctuating business and market conditions, or new federal regulations dictated software or system changes, clients would again rely on their consultants. In-house staff couldn't make the necessary adjustments because they'd never been clued in to what the consultants did or how they did it. Even companies with in-house IT staffers were likely to discourage tinkering for fear of "breaking" the new system. Of course, consultants really learned to like a model in which clients were wholly dependent upon their services.

Accounting firms had effectively convinced companies to hire their own consulting groups to implement costly, cumbersome projects. It seems they had taken Ross Perot's mantra—that the money is in software, and not in hardware, to heart. That so much of that software, once sold, was destined for the shelfware pile was irrelevant to the consulting firms. And you can rest assured that the accountants came up with a creative way to represent that investment on the balance sheet.

Eventually, as potential conflicts of interest between the accounting firms' auditing functions and their dynamic IT implementation imperatives became obvious, the marriage between accounting and IT consulting came to an end. Under myriad competitive and regulatory pressures, consolidation swept the industry, and the Big Eight ultimately dwindled to the Big Four. The era in which outsized IT software consulting firms commanded $100 million for a three-year, global SAP package implementation ended. Without producing measurable, positive business results, these companies couldn't survive. Two-year, $30 million customized CRM implementations proved valueless when sales forces refused to adopt the systems. (Perhaps it's no wonder the systems go unused—Accenture executive John Freeland's, *The Ultimate CRM*, is a 300-plus page tome, while Paul Greenberg's CRM book is particularly daunting at over 600 pages. We could implement an entire CRM system in the time it takes to read either of these books).

It is true that Accenture, BearingPoint, IBM Global Services, and CapGemini remain vital. But they are no longer business software consulting firms in the true sense. Their revenues and profits come primarily from IT infrastructure consulting. They address storage, backup and recovery, security, identification management, e-commerce infrastructure, disaster recovery, hosting, systems management—almost anything but the kind of discrete software project that supports the business process and produces business results.

Even the few remaining packaged software players have stopped pushing their enterprise licensed software implementations. Now they offer their software as modular services or so-called quick implementation express packages. That, in turn, minimizes potential profit for firms like IBM and CapGemini, which had formerly handled those implementations. That's why we call those firms dinosaurs.

Even with a shift in focus to IT infrastructure, the descendents of the Big Eight are battling to survive in the face of competition from low cost offshore outsourcing firms like Wipro and Infosys. With more competition springing up from Mumbai to Belarus, and Manila to Beijing, many are racing to open their own offshore development centers in hopes that salvation lies in outsourcing. This rationale requires consulting firms to sell clients on the merits of outsourcing datacenters, AP/AR, and HR departments—or any other functions that might be done better and cheaper overseas. Pundits have hailed this "business process outsourcing" (BPO) as the wave of the future. Whether BPO actually produces better long-term business results—and whether it is actually cheaper—remains to be seen. For now, though, the money is flowing in the outsourcers' direction.

There is ample evidence, however, that in many cases outsourcing—especially offshore outsourcing—saves little, if any money. Companies still require onsite employees with an intimate understanding of the enterprise and its available technology to define business needs and write specifications in terms that offshore developers can execute. Likewise, testing the prototype software, and determining how well it meets specifications and business requirements, necessarily falls to in-house staffers. And it takes local employees to train staff to use the software, ensure adoption, and maintain the system over time, as business and market changes dictate. Outsourcing and offshoring simply move a chunk of work to a lower cost location, in a form of geographic labor arbitrage. But the practices don't necessarily answer the problems of cost or manpower. The companies that once outsourced to Nebraska now offshore to Mumbai; tomorrow Belarus, Nairobi, or Cairo, may be in vogue. But except for those companies making long-haul investments in infrastructure overseas, the cost advantages of these locations are temporary. Salaries for IT professionals in India have steadily risen as demand outstrips availability; moreover, talented developers often choose to work for prestigious multinational companies. That can leave smaller enterprises with a less experienced or agile pool from which to hire—a hidden cost that's rarely considered.

The key point here comprises our Fourth Law of Consulting Economics: *Outsourcing is not consulting.* In fact, outsourcing often runs counter to the goals of consulting. Instead of helping an organization perform a task meant to achieve a certain business result, as consulting would, outsourcing involves giving up the task entirely, and hoping others will do it successfully. The focus is on the task and its cost, not the business result.

Of course, a company can never really wash its hands of the task, despite the promise of—and payment for—its worry-free completion. As we noted, specification development, testing, implementation, employee training, and system maintenance are just some of the tasks that must continue in-house. But companies that confuse the functions of outsourcing with consulting, and rely solely on the former, will miss out on the advantages of the latter. And good consultants can be invaluable when it comes to successfully navigating a new implementation, for instance, and learning how to take over and maintain a new system.

This leads us to a corollary to our Fourth Law of Consulting Economics: *Consulting, especially software consulting, is the process of helping companies to own their tasks, improve performance, and take advantage of new technologies to automate their tasks for the purpose of achieving specific business results.* That is the big difference from what the outsourcers and the descendents of the Big Eight are doing these days.

So, where does all this leave companies that need help implementing software to support their key business processes and deliver results? That's where we are heading. Read on.

3

The Last Hurrah: The Dotcom Boom and Bust

Here is one last digression before we talk about the state of software consulting today; it's a detour that underscores why we need the sort of software consulting revolution we call for in this book.

The dotcom boom was a classic economic bubble. Capital poured in for all sorts of online ventures thanks to speculation about the enormous potential for long-term financial payoff; those fronting it demanded results fast. That people sincerely thought the advent of the Internet changed something fundamental about the nature of business and its underlying economics may have amplified the magnitude of the bust. We've since collectively learned that certain business fundamentals—like cultivating a sound business plan, intelligent budgetary management, and targeted growth—are immutable. But it is true that the Internet changed *how* companies conducted business, by opening up a vast new media with virtually unlimited potential for breakthroughs in communication, information gathering, and commerce, to name a few. With those boons came new responsibilities and challenges—such as the secure management of vast amounts of sensitive data. Many pioneering internet entrepreneurs understood both the promises and challenges of doing business in the online frontier, at least on a theoretical level. But in the enthusiastic rush to beat out competition and establish an internet presence, few realized the timing may have been wrong. The same nascent technology that could help companies achieve deeper market penetration also enabled them to overreach or misappropriate resources, and make bigger, more devastating mistakes. And, because infrastructure of the online environment was still under development, internet entrepreneurs—who were essentially attempting to build on an uncompleted foundation—couldn't always deliver on business promises.

We see parallels between the early days of internet enterprise and the burgeoning auto industry in the early 20th century. Like the internet, the automobile embodied technology that promised previously unforeseen conveniences, along with lifestyle and business changes. Strides in mass production meant consumers had ever-greater accessibility to the automobile. And consumer demand encouraged speculators to jump into the auto-making fray; Detroit was home to well over 100 automakers by the 1920's. (In fact, the companies that have sprung up to leverage and dominate the Internet since 2000—Google, eBay, Salesforce.com, and more—remind us of the emergence of the Big Three automakers.)

Just as the auto industry paved the way for ancillary specialists like mechanics, the traffic on the information superhighway gave consulting companies the opportunity to capitalize on the dotcom craze. Alongside established, conventional IT firms, such as Cambridge Technology Partners, new consulting companies like Razorfish, Viant, and Sapient sprang up to specialize in internet technology. As slews of Internet and e-commerce boutiques made their home on the web, many turned to ad agencies, and design firms that had likewise turned their focus to online enterprises. These companies didn't always know much about IT, but they created slick visuals for nascent websites. Retrospectively, we question whether these websites truly served the business needs of the client. But at the time, the objective was to launch websites that looked sexy and exciting, based on the assumption that aesthetics would draw page views—and revenue. As we mentioned before, most of the consulting firms were project focused. So once a site was up and running, these firms had generally moved on to other projects. That lack of a long view didn't help the firms or their clients. As it became apparent that consulting firms were floundering, investors' confidence declined. Most of the new consulting firms that emerged during this period cared only about the short term, and the money they were making. They didn't understand what clients really needed, and they didn't amount to much in the end.

Andres Gillies, writing in *Forbes* magazine in Oct. 2000 summed up the situation as it looked at that time:

> It has been a rough couple of months for stocks of Internet consulting companies. Former stars like Razorfish now trade at a fraction of their 52-week highs.
>
> "The fourth quarter is not going to be an easy one for this group of stocks either," warns Steven Birer, senior e-services analyst at Robertson Stephens.
>
> Robert St. Jean, Internet and information technology services analyst at J.P. Morgan, points to several sector difficulties, including a drop-off in information technology spending by both dot-com and legacy companies, heavy staff turnover brought on by underwater stock options, and pressure to reduce fees. "When that sense of urgency goes away," St. Jean notes," clients tend to be a little more price sensitive."
>
> St. Jean thinks that the industry's problems are short term in nature and will be offset by new demands...

As it turned out, the industry's problems weren't exactly short term, though many dotcoms were able to sustain the illusion of viability, at least for as long as it took to spend millions in venture capital. Ironically, tough times for dotcoms meant business for the consulting firms, who were often called upon to implement full scale ERP and core business processing systems. After all, even companies producing low revenues hoped to stay afloat, ride out the downturn, and ultimately generate the sort of profits that had attracted their investors in the first place. Those that still had venture capital money to spend put their faith in technology, and hoped new software could save them.

Ultimately, countless internet start-ups collapsed. Conventional companies that had gotten swept up in the Internet spending frenzy took the bust as a warning; many spent the next few years recovering from their IT systems investment hangovers. In the meantime, though the technology industry faced an economic slowdown while the market corrected itself, real business growth was actually leading to new systems demand. By the time companies were prepared to start spending again on IT support, however, many of the consulting companies that had sprung up to capitalize on Internet-related IT spending had disappeared or been absorbed by other firms.

We saw all of this unfold, and applied the lessons we learned when we started Bluewolf. These lessons formed the basis for our Laws of Consulting Economics, which we will continue to define throughout this book. These principles aren't exactly rocket science—in fact, many are quite intuitive. But when we set out to establish Bluewolf, it seemed nobody recognized or practiced them. Today, many still don't. Here, we share the underpinnings of Bluewolf's guiding philosophy:

> The top priority is the customer and its business objectives.

> Listening—well—to what the customer says is essential. So is understanding that what they say and what they really mean are not necessarily the same. The ability to help a client reconcile what they are saying with the needs they are communicating is one of the primary ways the consultant adds value.

> Measurable results—not technology or projects—are the goal, and define success.

> Nothing happens until the customer has defined his or her success factors for every phase of every project.

> Always deliver measurable value, and do so expediently.

> Communicate, communicate, communicate! Ensure that sure the customer hears—and understands—what you're saying. And make sure you hear and understand what the customer is saying.

> Price consulting services based on the business value actually delivered (not promised) as defined by the client's success factors.

> Prepare the customer from day one to carry on after your departure.

We are convinced that if consulting firms had heeded these values during the dotcom craze, they would have saved their customers millions, instead of wasting that money on systems and technology that failed to deliver sufficient, if any, business value. These were our guiding principles when we started Bluewolf, and we hope they will form the backbone for a new breed of software consulting firm—one that is customer focused, business results-driven, and value-based.

The problem we faced back then was the lack of effective models, especially since most were reliant on inflexible software that, once installed, sat sputtering in corporations waiting for the next upgrade to really make things better. The dominant consulting model based on the waterfall development methodology didn't serve the consulting process we envisioned. After sifting through the debris of the dotcom bust and the ERP fiasco we stumbled on agile development methodologies, iterative prototyping, and extreme programming. These were hard-core software development concepts that were just starting to gain credence and visibility. We believed they could be applied to software consulting and software implementation.

The result could be called extreme or iterative consulting for agile businesses. And we decided to focus on agile businesses, or those businesses that understood the need to be prepared for rapid and frequent change. The reason is simple. Only if management is committed to creating an agile business is a company likely to survive in our 21st century global economy. Thus, we created a software consulting methodology for agile businesses; nothing else makes sense.

4

Back to the Future: The Emergence of Agile Consulting

In this chapter, we'll describe the advent of agile development and how we came to apply it to software consulting. We will compare it to the conventional world of software consulting and explain what is different about what we do. We don't want you to skip this chapter (we promise there are juicy details to come!), but we can distill what is unique about the pros of agile consulting into two major concepts:

1. **Agile consulting promises fast results.**

2. **It fosters client self-sufficiency.**

Agile development is an intriguing phenomenon that sprouted up in the IT subculture, and quietly worked its way into the mainstream with little fanfare. It started to attract attention in the mid 1990s when Kent Beck, Ward Cunningham, and Ron Jeffries first revealed their work on a payroll project entitled the Chrysler Comprehensive Compensation System. They called their approach "Extreme Programming," or "XP."

Beck defines XP in his book *Extreme Programming Explained: Embrace Change* (Addison-Wesley, 2000) as "a lightweight, efficient, low-risk, flexible, predictable, scientific, and fun way to develop software." We'd like to highlight XP's utility in mitigating the risks associated with software development.

It's a rare IT manager who isn't painfully aware of software development risks. Typical corporate software projects frequently run over budget, past deadline, and/or suffer from high rates of defects. Many ultimately fail to solve the business problem they were designed to address. In its *Research Note TU-11-0029,* the Gartner Group pointed out "more than 80 percent of IS-related projects are late, over budget, lacking in functionality or never delivered."

Other analysts, ranging from KPMG Canada to The Conference Board in New York, to Robbins-Gioia published reports throughout the late 1990s and early 2000-2001 showing failure rates of 40%, 50%, even 60%. It got to the point where it seemed like piling on; everybody seemed ready to beat up IT for high failure rates. have published similar findings:

The Standish Group International, http://www.standishgroup.com, tracked software development success and failure for a decade through its widely recognized CHAOS reports. In the first CHAOS report, published in 1994, the success rate was a dismal 16%. Nearly a decade later, in 2003, the success rate had reached only 31%. It stills publishes the CHAOS reports, which are available through its CHAOS Knowledge Center although we haven't seen one lately.

Granted, the above figures reflected assessment of a variety of issues; some analyses measured internal application development projects, while others dealt with enterprise software implementation and deployment efforts. The surveys in question used different methodologies, and comparisons were based on different benchmarks. Still, the overall message is unmistakably clear: Software development and implementation are high-risk, long-odds undertakings with elusive success rates. Squeamish bettors or prudent managers aren't likely to embrace these projects with enthusiasm—especially given the poor 10-year improvement rate demonstrated by the CHAOS reports. To be fair, even if they aren't clear-cut successes, most business software projects aren't abject failures either. They may come in later than planned and cost more than estimated, but their deployment tends to deliver at least some business value—even if they don't meet all expectations. Managers understand that risk is part of business, but we question whether there has to be so much risk associated with what are often pretty routine software development projects. After all, we're not talking about creating radically innovative software meant to map the known universe, model the human genome, or drive a top secret anti-ballistic missile system. To the contrary, we're talking about projects that produce software to handle mundane business processes, such as routine financial transactions, customer tracking, schedule production, and sales processing. (Remember that the first XP project, the Chrysler project, was a compensation system—albeit a big one for a complex organization.) Business managers have known how to handle these functions for ages, and were doing them long before the advent of computers. So we wonder why software meant to simplify and streamline these processes should create such headaches for users.

The goal of the XP effort, wrote Beck, was to "invent a style of software development that addresses these risks." To that end, he devised a system that called for short development cycles and required fast, continuing feedback to the developers. His system was incremental and iterative from the start, and presumed that projects would continually evolve. Frequent testing and regular communications—not only among the development team, but between developer and client—was essential. In fact, business clients are essentially part of the team on every XP project, and are tasked with writing the short tests for validating each piece of functional code. And XP programmers are expected to write the code together in pairs—actually sitting side by side at the same workstation.

At its inception, many considered XP quite radical. Some programmers still balk at the pair programming model and at the frequent communication, collaboration, and testing. Stereotypically, the best programmers have been lone wolves. But XP never required programming geniuses; in fact, Beck designed it expressly for "programmers with ordinary skills." Business managers, too, have taken issue with XP's expectation of their close, hands-on, business involvement. Beck acknowledged this resistance, when he wrote "XP frightens or angers some people who encounter it for the first time," yet he maintained "none of the ideas in XP are new." That's true. Experiments in agile and iterative development inspired the XP variation.

Craig Larman demystified the approach in *Agile & Iterative Development: A Manager's Guide* (Addison-Wesley, 2004), explaining "Iterative development is an approach to building software (or anything) in which the overall lifecycle is composed of several iterations in sequence. Each iteration is a self-contained mini-project composed of activities such as requirements analysis, design, programming, and test." Each iteration is intended to produce "a stable, integrated, and tested...system." So, though each iteration will ultimately contribute to a more complex system and greater functionality, each also delivers recognizable business value on it own.

In 2001, proponents of the various adaptive software development methodologies formed the Agile Alliance (www.agilealliance.com). Ditching the term "lightweight" in favor of "agile," the group noted that common to the various development approaches in question was an emphasis on "close collaboration between the programmer team and business experts; face-to-face communication (as more efficient than written documentation); frequent delivery of new deployable business value; tight, self-organizing teams; and ways to craft the code and the team such that the inevitable requirements churn was not a crisis."

The Agile Alliance published the "Manifesto for Agile Software Development," which can be found on its website and reads as follows:

Manifesto for Agile Software Development

We are uncovering better ways of developing software by doing it and helping others do it. Through this work we have come to value:

Individuals and interactions *over processes and tools*

Working software *over comprehensive documentation*

Customer collaboration *over contract negotiation*

Responding to change *over following a plan*

That is, while there is value in the items on the right, we value the items on the left more.

Kent Beck	James Grenning	Robert C. Martin
Mike Beedle	Jim Highsmith	Steve Mellor
Arie van Bennekum	Andrew Hunt	Ken Schwaber
Alistair Cockburn	Ron Jeffries	Jeff Sutherland
Ward Cunningham	Jon Kern	Dave Thomas
Martin Fowler	Brian Marick	

The signatories also outline a list of principles that elaborate on the manifesto, but these four points capture the essence of the initiative. Philosophically, we align pretty closely with the Agile Alliance's manifesto, though we've got additional guiding principles of our own. We're fanatical about defining specific success criteria, and about backing those criteria with a satisfaction guarantee. We'll talk more about those points in later chapters, but for now, we'd like to look more closely at how agile development works.

The key to agile development is a practice called timeboxing, in which each iteration is built within a well-defined period, or "timebox." Large projects are broken down into discrete segments that can be built, tested, and delivered in a defined, short time period. Typically, these projects last between two to six weeks. Deadlines are firm, but there is room to alter or scale back the deliverables in a given timebox. This practice gives the end-user quick access to new software as it is developed. Plus, timeboxing not only preserves or enhances the client's productivity, it means feedback can be offered based on actual use of the software while it's still in process. Other aspects of the agile approach we find very appealing include:

> The focus on simplicity;
> That there is open access and full transparency for project management and other pertinent project data;
> That we work with empowered and self-directed teams;
> That frequent feedback allows the flexibility to both expect and invite change and adaptation;
> That we gather requirements through face-to-face communication.

Like many in the IT field in the late 1990's, we were flummoxed by the dotcom bust, the ERP software/shelfware dilemma, and all of the consulting industry confusion that characterized the period. Fortunately, we realized that using agile development, extreme programming, and associated methodologies could help us navigate our nascent consulting firm through it all. We used small teams that communicated frequently and directly, worked closely with the customers, and focused on small sets of functionality that would deliver business value within a timebox. And we took an iterative approach to ensure responsiveness to change. This worked not only for custom software development, but also for implementing or modifying existing software packages.

On top of that we realized that, together with the business client, we could define very specific, measurable results and guarantee the delivery of those results. We ensured flexibility by dispatching small teams, and empowered them to deal directly with the client, make changes on the fly, and be self-managing. Working this way, we could deliver tangible business results without compromising our own profitability.

We were able to provide extreme, agile, iterative business software consulting, and have since embraced it as our Fifth Law of Consulting Economics: *Make agile methodology your consulting practice model.*

We've done just that in over 1000 customer engagements, and we can assure you: agile consulting works. It is truly a win-win situation for everyone involved.

We feel pretty fortunate for discovering that we could apply agile development to consulting—especially when most large consulting companies were embracing offshore development and moving their knowledge centers to countries far, far away. So why haven't the big consulting houses like Accenture and Deloitte woken up to the agile phenomenon (which would enable them stay close to home, where rates are high, and managing the business is infinitely easier)?

Here is the answer: Agile and iterative development threatens their business model, which depends on long projects, keeping consultants embedded with customers for years on end, and cloaking projects so that clients can never take the helm and control their own software destiny.

Agile promotes the opposite philosophy. It's desirable that clients see results fast, and become self-sufficient through involvement in the development process. Moreover, we've found that clients often learn quickly, and gain the confidence to take on many aspects of development themselves. If delivering a complex software project is like getting 1,000 people to do the Hustle, in unison, on a dance floor, Agile is like taking small groups of those people, in threes or fours, showing them the steps, and then integrating the small groups until all 1,000 have it down. The dance instructors step aside and let the early dancers teach the rest of the group the new moves.

This is huge. Traditional consulting firms have no desire to see their clients succeed without them. From their perspective, it is more advantageous to sit in meetings mapping out every step for each of the 1,000 dancers, before blindfolding them and leading them through the dance, months later. This is a key reason that there's typically a misalignment between the traditional consulting firm's and its client's ideas of success. In direct contrast, we believe that a self-sufficient client can better run its business, and can ultimately provide the best, most credible testament to the value we add.

Does our model presuppose a goal to put ourselves out of business on every project? Perhaps. That's why conventional consulting firms find our approach scary. But we refuse to manage our business based on fear, or to employ the tricks of deception that lead to the misalignment with client needs that most consulting firms foster. Instead, we'd rather have faith in our ability to deliver value quickly, and the confidence that doing so will lead to more and more engagements. So far, that formula has worked. We already have thousands of engagements under our belts and confidence that our past successes will breed future ones. Rather than putting us out of business, agile consulting helps us attract ever more clients who want to learn to dance.

5

Iterate or Die: Extreme Consulting for Agile Business

In 1999, the turn of the millennium was looming, and companies were scrambling to implement new Y2K-compliant enterprise software packages. Back then, we were still working for traditional service companies, which were profiting handsomely thanks to expensive implementation projects and over-engineered solutions.

At the time, we certainly weren't complaining about the size of our paychecks. But we were becoming less and less enthralled with the IT consulting climate, and noticed that customers were, too. Clients started to quietly grumble about cost, quality, and return on investment of their IT projects.

Then, by the end of 2000, everyone's focus shifted to the tanking stock market. Companies were universally tightening their belts, and many sent armies of consultants packing. We'd like to think we were prescient, but that wasn't the case. We weren't heroes or whistler blowers. We didn't run around predicting gloom and disaster like some IT Cassandra. We did sense, however, that the software universe was poised to undergo a fundamental shift in the way software was implemented, deployed and maintained. We were lucky enough to quickly pull $200,000 out of our various personal investments, which were nose-diving along with everyone else's. With that money we bootstrapped ourselves a new type of consulting firm. We did it in a climate that had become distinctly inhospitable to consulting firms in general. Needless to say, raising venture capital was not an option.

We rented an office for $1,500 a month—complete with a tiny unisex bathroom, with a knee-hitting stall door. We furnished the office with two metal desks pillaged from a flea market, and bought our first phone system at Staples. We spent the next five months jiggling the phone chord, to manage the static (hint: don't buy a cheap phone). And we cold called every CIO and IT executive for whom we could find a phone number.

Our calls, however, were different from the usual consultant calls. We weren't prescribing any solutions, grand or otherwise. We were asking questions and listening to the answers. And we connived our way into offices whenever possible, so that we could see their faces, and their offices, and hear their pain, and assess how we might be able to help.

Our first meeting ever took place in January 2001, eight days into our existence. Michael cold called Olympus, the camera company, and reached an IT executive who muttered something about a failed Siebel project.

"We're in your neighborhood tomorrow, " Michael said, "and we'll stop by at 10:00 a.m."

"Sure."

"Great. See you then."

Lesson number 1: Keep it short and simple, and get in front of the customer before he or she can say no. That was our approach.

When we drove out to Olympus' Long Island office the next day, fighting traffic and a snowstorm, we were embarking on a journey that would take us much further than we imagined. At that point, all we knew was that our LLC had been filed and our office keys worked (even if the radiator leaked and rattled and gave off way too much heat). Now we were hunting for our first piece of business. We had no idea what we were going to say to this IT executive who surely forgot we were coming, and were startled when the receptionist called his office and said "two gentlemen from Bluewolf are here to see you." At least she referred to us as gentlemen.

What happened next still makes us laugh today. And it offers clues to what was going on in the consulting world at that time and how much confusion was driving (or thwarting) the software consulting marketplace.

"Bring me up-to-date on Bluewolf," said the IT executive, across the conference room table. Up-to-date? What in the hell was this guy talking about, we wondered? We had just started the company! So right there, in front of a total stranger who assumed we had been around for years, we started spinning the story of a new consulting model and expert resources and quick deliverables. We suggested he let us take useless software off his hands piece by piece, so that he could start to report some progress to his superiors. Talk about flying by the seat of our pants! As we pitched and listened, it became clear that for years, Olympus had been stymied by countless enterprise software and consulting "solutions" that never met the company's needs. They'd been victimized by a lack of transparency, in a market that thrived on cultivating confusion. We're not sure if this poor executive mistook our fledgling company for one that had been in business for years, or if he was just disheartened or desperate enough about the state of their IT systems to talk to us. We never closed the Olympus deal. In fact, we don't think we even secured a second meeting. But we learned that day, and from similar meetings over the next several months, that hundreds of companies were unhappy with the state of their IT systems. None used the word "success" when describing project outcomes.

In Bluewolf's first year, while we rose to profitability and learned the basics of our new model, we closed only a handful of projects. Still, people were listening. More importantly, we were listening closely to them. Over and over, we heard that companies were sick of the consulting firms of the past. Our confidence and vision began to grow.

We met IT executives at companies big and small, and kept asking questions. "What are you going to do now?" "What do you need now to move forward?" And they started to tell us.

What we heard didn't exactly surprise us. They had invested in software nobody was using, or that didn't work optimally. Or the business had changed, and the software couldn't respond. Then they started asking us: "What should we do now?"

At the time, our idea was to apply a few really astute technical resources to salvage usability from whatever software they had, and to make it work fast. That's what the CIOs wanted—something that would deliver quick business value to their users. They were not worried about big plans or grandiose architecture. We were small and could work fast.

We weren't exactly sure how we would deliver. We hadn't yet recognized the potential of agile methodologies. But we knew exactly what we would NOT do. We would:

> - **NOT develop detailed project plans that mapped out every twist and turn in excruciating detail;**
> - **NOT write excessive documentation;**
> - **NOT allow the all-powerful project manager—who'd enforce cumbersome policies and procedures, while hindering responsiveness and innovation—to even touch the projects;**
> - **NOT follow detailed methodologies;**
> - **NOT undertake any IT-centric projects.**

Basically, we declared the Sixth Law of Consulting Economics: *Throw out the rules.* We declared the days of overpriced, underperforming software implemented by overpaid, under-producing consultants were over. Instead, we launched a consulting practice based on:

> - **Frameworks (as opposed to methodologies), or loose structures that could be easily and quickly adapted to a given situation;**
> - **Constant dialog with the customer, via frequent conversations in real time, face-to-face, and over the phone;**
> - **Fast deliverables (typically in 30, 60, or 90 days);**
> - **Iterating—or trying things out;**
> - **Emphasizing business value only, without promoting IT for its own sake.**

"Iterate or die" became our bywords. We were working with CIOs stuck with bloated software that didn't meet their business needs, and often didn't work at all. We focused on creating functionality, iterating like mad until the customer had something useful and productive. Compared to what these CIOs had experienced before—armies of consultants who camped out in their offices for months or years on end, seemingly laying siege to their organization and still not delivering any useful software—our fast, iterative approach saved their lives, or at least their jobs. (After all, CIO's weren't immune to layoffs in the wake of the dotcom bust.)

It took awhile before we saw the parallels between our business software consulting style and the agile or XP approach to hardcore application development and coding. When we finally connected the dots we understood what "iterate or die" really was: Agile consulting.

6
The Software Conundrum

The volatile IT climate of the late 1990's, and the subsequent dotcom bust left organizations faced with what can only be described as a software conundrum. How, business managers and CIOs asked, could they obtain reasonably priced software in a timely fashion that would produce ongoing business value? Clearly the approaches of the past didn't work, as demonstrated by the millions of dollars in shelfware they had sitting around their offices.

Budgetary constraints compounded the problem. The country was sliding into a recession, and economists were theorizing about the possibility of a depression. Businesses were exhorting managers to do more with fewer funds. Except perhaps in cases where new systems were needed urgently, managers were adverse to spending money on new software, systems, and applications—especially if they'd previously wasted resources on highly touted systems that failed to deliver business value. Companies needed workable software and new functionality if they were to effectively compete in a highly competitive, rapidly globalizing marketplace, so software updates were inevitable. But managers found most software choices utterly unappealing. They'd already been burned by big-ticket ERP systems. They rejected canned applications that invariably required businesses to conform their processes to the software. Customized software could theoretically do a better job of meeting a company's needs, but its development took far too long, was prohibitively expensive, and didn't guarantee business value.

Every option, CIOs and business managers told us, looked like quicksand. This led to the Seventh Law of Consulting Economics: *When facing quicksand, steer clear of it.* That may seem obvious advice, but how do you determine if what you're looking at is actually quicksand? How do you make educated choices without becoming paralyzed by fear of a misstep? Chances are, a company will get mired in metaphorical quicksand when it embraces the idea that the power of a proposed IT solution lies with technology. In contrast, companies that understand their power unquestionably lies with their people and business processes tend to make the far safer choice to focus on systems that support those people and processes.

So let's take a look at the primary options from the standpoint of the Seventh Law:

> - **Custom application development is too slow, too costly, and leaves companies completely at the mercy of outside technologists. (Proposed software is often irrelevant to the company's actual needs; even if it works as promised, it isn't usually flexible enough to evolve with the business. That's a shame, because by the time it's delivered, it may be obsolete).**

> - **Integrated enterprise software packages are a close cousin of custom developed applications. As such, they are associated with all the same costs, delays, and problems of custom development—minus the advantage of customization.**

> - **Developing applications in-house is a proven way for companies to get exactly the functionality they want without entailing high licensing fees. This can be a better way to ensure that the focus remains on the business and its people. However, companies still face the challenge of making sure that the application and business teams work closely together. Moreover, the "build-your-own" approach still requires a tremendous time investment, as the conventional software development and testing process is slow, no matter who does it. And though licensing and maintenance fees are circumvented, hiring staff to develop, test, and deploy the applications—and providing them the software tools to do the job—is often quite costly.**

As we discussed before, the big consulting firms have historically bankrolled their operations by successfully selling their clients on the merits of the first two options. The firms are no better (and probably much worse) than their clients at predicting what functionality those businesses will need in the future. They routinely deliver outdated software. But they get paid even if they deliver systems devoid of much business value, and likewise profit when clients request system changes to salvage function or reflect current needs. That's a major disincentive for change in practice, and gives the consulting firms power over their clients.

The integrated enterprise packaged application vendors took a slightly different approach, with similar results. They didn't pretend to understand how a particular business worked. They simply offered software that would support so-called industry proven best practices, whether those happened to be the company's practices or not. In effect, the software vendor was dictating how an organization should implement its processes and run its business. This one-size-fits-all approach dictated that every company would take orders and schedule production and service their customers the same way. Again, the power didn't lie with businesses' processes or its people.

The application vendors capitalized on companies' desire to adhere to industry-standard best practices. Business that found their processes didn't mesh with the new technology they deployed were likely to change their own practices—after all, what manager would admit they didn't follow best practices? How a business might actually differentiate itself from its competitors wasn't the vendors' concern—and it was something too many companies overlooked in the effort to conform their processes to their new technology.

Even savvy companies interested in adapting the software to better support their own practices had to hire a consultant or the vendor to customize the package. The only other option—though it wasn't a particularly good one—was to take a wait-and-see approach, and hope that the vendor might eventually work a desired enhancement into some future version. Of course, customizing the application had its downside, too, because the investment was lost the moment a company upgraded to the vendor's next release. If the original customization utilized the vendor's application programming interface (API), it was sometimes possible to salvage some of it, but there were no guarantees this would work.

The build-your-own option essentially puts companies—whose core competencies generally lie elsewhere—into the software development business. But hiring, motivating, and retaining good software developers is a challenge, and software development is a high-risk undertaking. Unless the businesses are seriously committed to this effort, they tend to run into trouble. Many organizations have elected to dismantle their in-house software development operations to focus on their core business and their true core competencies.

In response to critical press about hundred-million dollar software deployments that failed to deliver, the packaged application vendors did two things: they introduced quick and easy deployment packages, and re-architected their applications. The long-term goal of the re-architecture initiatives was to restructure monolithic code into a service-oriented architecture (SOA). We are great fans of SOA, and believe that big packaged application vendors are on the right track, and may yet turn out some useful SOA-based software. At the same time, we wonder if other programming advances might supplant SOA before then. We're also realists, and recognize that either way, companies need software now to run their businesses.

The express easy-to-deploy packages come with graphical wizards to guide users through a standard implementation. The wizards work, but result in cookie-cutter implementations meant to ensure industry-standard best practices, without regard for variations in processes and operations among individual businesses. Companies get stuck with software that doesn't address their actual needs; as we discussed before, this focus on technology robs companies of the power that should inherently lie in their business and with their staff. Cost and deployment speed make express packages seem attractive, but they're quicksand just the same. We recommend steering clear of them.

Finally, it's no surprise that software is expensive—it always has been. Beyond licensing fees, maintenance, and consulting expenses, big applications require a commensurate application infrastructure—often with dedicated servers and databases, including backup and recovery, and people with the specialized technical skills to deploy, manage, and maintain that infrastructure.

So how can companies best solve this software conundrum? As you might guess, we advocate using an iterative approach, or what Adam Bosworth, the Vice President of Engineering at Google, has described as "intelligent reaction." At the Salesforce Dreamforce '05 Conference, in a presentation titled Intelligent Reaction Bosworth described the concept this way: "most educated people... are aware that evolution is not about intelligent design...it is a reaction to the environment, doing those things that cause you to survive better than your competitors and evolve accordingly. Well, software is evolving in the same way right now—it is not about intelligent design, it is about intelligent reaction. It is about figuring out what works for people..."

Software that incorporates intelligent reaction is built by business savvy people. They observe what is happening in the real world of the business, consider the software users, try new things in response to what they see, learn from the reaction, and iterate again and again. In keeping with our Seventh Law, this is software focused solely on what the people and the business need and do. It is software that will work for a company or will quickly change until it does, and it can keep evolving along with the business. This kind of software, based on intelligent reaction, is used today by much admired companies like Google, eBay, and Yahoo. Bosworth's idea of intelligent reaction extends to consulting too. We call it agile consulting.

7

The People Paradox: Who Will Do the Work?

In the downturn that followed the dotcom bust, IT work-ers throughout the industry found themselves out of work. It wasn't just the IT world that was impacted by the flagging economy—in most business sectors, companies felt enormous pressure to reduce overhead in an effort to contend with new global competitors. Mass layoffs ensued, and many companies reduced benefits for their remaining workers. In an effort to become lean and flexible, companies gravely undermined the social contract between employee and employer.

In the meantime, as their clients scaled back their own budgets, IT con-sulting firms could no longer sustain the enormous staffs they'd employed on large-scale projects like ERP implementations. Most consulting firms were similarly structured; they maintained an army of technical special-ists and administrative support people working under a small group of senior partners, who often served as strategic project team leaders. But as companies reevaluated the vogue for expensive system overhauls and software implementations, many concluded that earlier investments had yielded underwhelming returns—and plenty of shelfware. Demand for the services of the IT consulting old guard dropped considerably.

Though layoffs seemed a necessary cost-cutting measure, many businesses erred by overzealously downsizing their IT departments. With work to be done and no one to do it, CIOs began complaining. Concurrent advances in the technology that supported global communications seemed to offer a viable solution. Offshore outsourcing began to look like a very attractive solution to companies' staffing problems.

After all, companies were already accustomed to having IT work done remotely. Proponents of offshore outsourcing argued that it didn't matter if the specialists completing that work were situated in Chatham, New Jersey or Mumbai, India. Of course, they also pointed out that the technical specialist churning out code in Mumbai would do it for 20% less than a local contractor. The promise of a seemingly infinite supply of skilled IT workers—who were accessible via the Internet, and who could be hired at low wages, seemed an unbeatable deal. Indeed, almost every big company today participates in some form of offshore outsourcing.

In a widely reported Gartner study, the research firm predicts that worldwide spending on offshore research, development, and engineering will increase by a stunning 860%, from $1.25 billion in 2004 to as much as $12 billion in 2010. In addition, Gartner also predicts that offshore spending on infrastructure outsourcing will grow from about $250 million in 2004 to as much as $4 billion by 2010. Offshore spending on application-development services during the same time will more than double from $23 billion to about $50 billion.

In terms of IT employment in North America, the offshoring predictions don't translate into an encouraging picture:

> **Analysts at Moors & Cabot predict that 30% of IT jobs will ultimately move offshore, although it will take more than a decade, maybe two.**

> **Forrester Research predicts that 3.4 million U.S. services jobs— including a number of IT-related positions—will move offshore by 2015.**

Between the dotcom bust—which quelled the dreams of 20-somethings hoping to get rich through a quick IPO—and the embrace of outsourcing, college students began turning away from IT careers. The enrollment and graduation rates in computer science and software engineering programs fell as students, discouraged by grim predictions of offshore-driven declines in IT employment, looked elsewhere for their futures. A smart, ambitious kid could do better in financial services, accounting, and law. Even if consulting firms or IT departments were hiring, there were fewer smart young people to recruit.

The thinning field should have been good news for students who ultimately earned computer science-related degrees. But as they tried to enter the workforce, they found that their training in modern programming with C++, Java, XML, and Active Server Pages left them unqualified for available jobs. That's because the IT departments at many big companies faced a different type of need as the people who had been caring for and feeding their core mainframe systems for 30 years started to hit retirement age. The IT data center veterans were grabbing what was left of their pensions, often encouraged by early retirement incentives intended to reduce overhead, and bailing out. Companies needed people with mainframe skills—like COBOL, IMS, and RACF. Internet whiz kids couldn't do the job even if they wanted it.

By 2003, the stock market had rebounded, the economy was healthier, and job prospects looked better for new IT graduates. CIOs—who had previously culled their staffs to bring costs into line—now worried about finding good people to staff their IT departments. Replacing the aging data center crowd was no longer the CIO's sole concern. Companies began to embrace the concept of "Web 2.0" (so named by O'Reilly and MediaLive International) and the notion of "the Web as platform" (which was elucidated during O'Reilly's first Web 2.0 Conference in 2004). Businesses developed new web-based business initiatives, and they needed employees who possessed the latest IT skills to execute those plans. But CIOs were hard-pressed to find talented programmers and engineers adept at working with the promising Web and SOA-related technologies. The trend toward layoffs during the economic downturn—rather than retraining and employee cultivation—deeply damaged workers' faith in traditional employer-employee compacts.

The next generation of computer whizzes was understandably wary, and had little interest in entering the corporate IT world. Now, students are savvy to the potential of Web 2.0, and are acculturated to an Internet populated by MySpace, Livejournal, and Napster. They don't aspire to corporate IT jobs—they're busy dreaming up the next YouTube.

Today CEOs and CIOs are facing a difficult challenge. Without a sufficient talent pool to draw on, and with pressure to keep overhead low so their companies can compete globally, how can they find the IT staffers they desperately need? Having lost their trust and goodwill during tougher economic times, how can companies find, retain, and motivate employees in an offshoring world? And is winning those people back a costly endeavor?

Now, let's go back to the big consulting firms. What were they doing while the corporate world was on the economic mend and students were veering away from IT? As businesses explored offshoring, many big consulting firms transitioned away from large-scale implementation projects and rebounded as well. They raced to set up development and support centers in India, China, and anywhere else they could find English-speaking IT workers who could be hired cheap. The firms' partners and top management typically stayed stateside, while their overseas hires remained on native soil. Because the high salaries of stateside consulting partners were offset by the lower wages paid to offshore workers, the arrangement enabled the firms to retain clients while remaining competitive with the offshore outsourcing vendors.

There were, however, problems with this approach. Communications between the clients and the people doing the actual work suffered. That's because clients relayed their needs to the partners, as they had always done, yet the firms didn't typically have effective interactions with their overseas hires. It was the equivalent of the kindergarten game of telephone, in which the children attempt to pass a message around a circle. Each child whispers the message exactly as she heard it to her neighbor, who passes it along in turn. By the time the message makes it back to the first child, it's usually completely garbled, and the kids are reduced to hysterics. Kids easily "get" the take-home lessons of the telephone game—that communication is key to getting a message across clearly, and that it's also sometimes tricky to achieve. Yet as they began their forays into offshoring, consulting firms often lost track of those lessons. For the clients whose business requirements, needs, and requests constituted the garbled messages in a game of offshoring telephone, the results were far from funny. Frustrated by how their requests were misunderstood and confused, many clients wished they could just sit down with the technical team and show them what they wanted in real time, hear how the team understood the instructions, answer their questions right on the spot, and correct misunderstandings immediately. Unfortunately, clients couldn't do that unless they were prepared to circumvent the consulting firm, and hop on a 16-hour flight to India whenever the need arose. Instead, most opted to wait weeks and often months to see a prototype or proof of concept. If something needed fixing, the game of telephone started again. A few rounds of that game were enough to make the most tolerant client want to jump on an airplane—even if that meant disrupting whatever was going on back at the office.

This brings us to our Eighth Law of Consulting Economics: *When it comes to success, communication is everything.* And we have a corollary to this one too: Not all communications are equal. Face-to-face and real-time communications beat email, fax, and FedEx every time.

In terms of offshoring, both distance and time-zone differences represent built-in barriers to achieving real-time communication, which can make it an undesirable option for many IT needs. But beyond that, offshoring isn't usually the bargain CIOs expected anyway. It may cost less to hire offshore versus stateside IT workers, but after retaining the services of an expensive consulting firm and hiring local staff, few companies realize the dramatic cost savings offshoring allegedly promises. Companies still need business savvy, skilled, IT-aware people to write the requirements and test the systems that come back from the offshore center, and to integrate those systems with existing or future ones. They need people to train users in those systems. Factor in periodic travel and other miscellaneous costs—including those associated with finding, hiring, and retaining local staff—and any anticipated savings have been eaten up. There is, however, a different model for getting the work done. We'll discuss it in detail later. For now it involves the following:

> > Having the client do what it does best, which is to manage and refine its business processes;

> > Building a staff of business process experts who are IT-savvy (but who needn't be technology experts);

> > Parachuting in a selected few specialists (people who come onsite) for very specific, short duration situations;

> > Utilizing remote managed services providers for ongoing specialized technology needs.

Business processes define a company's identity. Those processes encapsulate the company's core competencies, competitive advantage, strategy, and vision. They should be hung onto at all costs.

Since business processes are so crucial, it is vital to invest in staff members who will be expert in shaping and managing those processes. Yes, they should be smart about IT, but they certainly needn't be technology experts. They should never be slaves to technology. Instead, the technology should serve the business processes.

Yes, there come times when businesses need technical expertise. But that doesn't mean it's necessary to have those experts on staff. It's a far better strategy to bring them in when necessary for exactly what needs to be done, and to send them away when the specific task is complete.

Ongoing technical tasks—like database administration or network management—may support business processes without representing a company's core competencies, in which case the people who handle those tasks needn't be on staff. That is what managed service providers are for. Companies that use them free themselves to focus on their business processes, without being distracted by technology.

8
The Rise
of the CPO

Without question, information technology systems are vital to modern businesses. IT tool use is practically hardwired into every business process, from communications to customer relationship management, from streamlining sales processes in order to enhance efficiency and productivity, to post-sale customer support. Companies also need IT tools to design and build their products, process transactions, monitor and manage their supply chains and business processes, and ensure compliance with a seemingly endless stream of government requirements and regulatory mandates.

In short, you can't do much without information systems. Imagine trying to run a company today without email! Customers, prospects, suppliers, and partners expect companies to have websites, and to be able to communicate with them promptly and efficiently via email. They expect orders processed, invoices sent, and payments posted reliably and accurately. It takes IT systems to expedite, facilitate, and manage the demand and opportunity process, the customer support process, and the product development and delivery processes. Practically every aspect of business has an IT component. Companies can't even hire and fire people—or even go out of business if that time comes, we suppose—without the use of IT systems.

Large, midsize, and small companies all need IT systems. But none of them should be forced into the IT business just to have access to the IT tools they need, any more than they should have to go into the power generation business in order to flip on the lights. It seems absurd to imagine a company running its own auto assembly lines just to have access to shipping trucks, or maintaining a paper mill in order to ensure a steady paper supply. Yet, companies repeatedly find themselves deeply involved in the IT business. They run large IT operations, manage teams of application software developers, and are constantly integrating, testing, and maintaining applications. Many also maintain groups dedicated to telecommunications. And they do all this despite the fact that their actual business—the source of their revenue and profits—lies completely outside the realm of IT.

Realistically, we don't believe companies will—or should—remove themselves completely from the IT industry. IT systems are too important to businesses, and they need to maintain some knowledge of how to deploy IT, maintain their systems, and train employees in their use. Furthermore, companies need to have access to IT-savvy people who know their business and their particular processes, and can guide them in getting the most from their IT system investments. Depending on the size of the organization, these may be people on staff or outsiders who are brought in as needed.

What most companies should not need to do, however, is build and maintain a large IT infrastructure. To be blunt, that isn't easy or cheap. Finding skilled IT people can be a challenge. As we pointed out previously, college students are not exactly flocking to careers in IT; those that do are often more interested in working with leading-edge technology, or in jobs that position them to play the IPO game. Few companies can offer those opportunities.

Even companies that manage to find promising candidates—and can afford to hire them—may discover that keeping them is a challenge. It doesn't take long before headhunters start knocking on the doors of talented employees. To retain good staff, companies should be prepared to offer better perks than the headhunters promise. In the attempt to outbid recruiters, companies may need to bow to employee requests to upgrade to a tantalizing new technology, or may have to throw their existing salary structure right out the window.

Employee salaries are only the start of the IT expenses, although probably the largest single chunk. Companies also need to factor in their investment in hardware and software. Moore's Law may indicate that as processor power increases, the cost of IT systems decreases, but those systems are pricey, nevertheless—both initially and over time. And it is not just primary systems and applications that are costly. So are the tools for application customization, integration, and systems management.

There are a few companies—such as Google, eBay, and Amazon. com—for which major investment in IT is strategic. These companies base their very existence on their IT prowess. Their IT systems generate their revenue and profits, and their IT innovation keeps competitors at bay. For these companies, the IT infrastructure is as central to their core business as assembly plants are to General Motors or oil refineries are to ExxonMobil.

Most companies, however, are different. They use IT, and may even incorporate it into their business processes to achieve or maintain their competitive advantage. But they needn't transform themselves into IT organizations merely to have access to the technology they need. There's little business sense in diverting funds that should support a company's core competencies into a major IT infrastructure investment.

When we speak with business executives, they report feeling distracted, restricted, or even imprisoned by IT. Dealing with IT-related issues diverts their attention from their actual businesses, business processes, and—most critically—away from their customers. For example, with every change in government regulations or tax laws, they have to assign staff to comb through their systems to ensure compliance. Dealing with IT issues distracts employees from the company's real business—be it footwear design, hydraulics, or transportation—and from serving the customer. The irony is that those very IT tools were meant to facilitate business operations and customer service efforts.

Part of the reason for this book, then, is to help managers get out of the IT business so they can focus on their real business. That's also the mission of Bluewolf. CEOs tell us that they don't want to be in the systems and telecom infrastructure or database management businesses, and they certainly don't want to be in the software development business. They want the benefits of IT systems and telecommunications. They want the benefits of databases and, more specifically, of the data they contain. They want the benefits of sophisticated software. They just don't want to be in the IT business.

Nevertheless, the CIO is an important position in any business. Someone needs to understand the organization's data and information systems, and know how to utilize and optimize them to advance the company's goals and strategies. The problem with the CIO position in most companies, however, is that often, the job description mandates the CIO to focus on technology and data. That, in turn, tends to pull the company into the technology sphere. To those holding hammers, every problem looks like a nail; good CIO's, when told their job is to find the best technology solution for every business problem, will do just that—whether technology is the best solution or not.

Remember our Second Law of Consulting Economics: *A successful business process trumps cool technology*? We believe good CIOs are invaluable, but believe that it's even more important that companies have what we call the Chief Process Officer (CPO). A business is a collection of its processes, not its IT systems. For a successful business, it is these processes that make the business unique, provide its competitive advantage, and keep its customers coming back. IT systems are great to the extent that they are embedded in, and facilitate the optimization of, a company's business processes. They should always service a company's strategies and goals. But it is critical to understand that the true heart of an organization lies in its core processes, and not in its IT systems.

That is why we advocate the idea of the CPO. It is the responsibility of the CPO to keep everyone focused on the organization's business processes, to change those that no longer work well or efficiently, and to develop new processes whenever there is a need or opportunity. It is the CPO who keeps everyone in the organization focused on what is unique about the business.

The idea of the business process encountered some heavy flack during the mid-1990s, following the publication of *Reengineering the*

Corporation: A Manifesto for Business Revolution, by Michael Hammer and James Champy. In the book, the authors introduced the concept of business process reengineering (BPR). Their contention was that companies had grown big and bloated and were badly in need of streamlining their business processes. Whether the authors intended it or not, managers who read the book seized on it as the justification for massive downsizing. Often, they downsized first, and rethought or reengineered the associated business processes later. Sometimes their rethinking only went so far as "do more with less." Without any reengineering of the business process at all, they simply expected fewer people to do the same work the same way. This mindless downsizing under the guise of BPR gave process management a bad name.

More recently, the concept has resurfaced under the labels "business process management" and "business process optimization." At its 2007 Business Process Management Summit in London, Gartner even helped export the concept to the European market. In its conference literature, Gartner described the rationale for business process management thus:

> *"Everyone talks about aligning IT with business. Business processes are where this happens—where the right technology can help evaluate, re-design, streamline, automate, integrate, monitor and improve the processes that determine the operational success of every enterprise.*
>
> *The theory of Business Process Management has been around for a while, but the practice is just starting to ramp up in some of Europe's most competitive companies. And the benefits are there for all to see: faster innovation, improved responsiveness, lower costs, happier customers, higher profits. You can't get more aligned with business than that."*

Nevertheless, business process management remains a somewhat vague concept today. We like this definition: A *business process* is a series of tasks or operations that perform what is considered a logically complete unit of work from a business standpoint, such as taking an order or pulling an item out of inventory and shipping it to the client. *Business process management* consists of a set of activities revolving around the planning and performance monitoring of a business process. Such business process management draws upon knowledge, experience, skills, tools, techniques, and technology to define, visualize, measure, control, report and improve the business processes with the goal of profitably meeting customer demand.

In short, business process management, or BPM, addresses and optimizes the sequence of steps it takes to perform a task for a customer. The task might be as simple as generating an invoice, or as complicated as taking an order and initiating a production request that triggers corresponding activities at three external partners. It might occur within a single functional silo, between several functional silos, or across different enterprises. Regardless, it is these processes that really define a business.

For example, a company that achieves a particularly efficient loan approval process might approve a typical consumer loan just 15 minutes—a distinct advantage in that market. Or, let's say it takes a company 90 days to fulfill a custom order via a 100-step production process; whether that time frame and process represents a competitive advantage depends entirely upon that particular market. Does the design and execution of the process allow the company to cut costs on the product or service end? Can it help provide customers far better support or quality than they are accustomed to? Whatever the processes, and whether they are good or bad, they define the business and, ultimately, its success.

The CPO, more than the CIO, is responsible for identifying, monitoring, managing, and optimizing business processes. Sometimes the task involves applying automation tools (IT) to the process. Just as likely, the task involves identifying bottlenecks that occur when a task is handed off from one person, function, or department to another. Maybe serial functions—activities that follow in sequence behind one another—can be performed in parallel, with those actions being performed simultaneously. The focus of the CPO may be on the individual task, but the goal is to improve business outcomes. The CPO needs to understand the ramifications of changing a process in terms of customer satisfaction and the achievement of company objectives. Where necessary, the CPO needs to step in, redesign, and automate processes to achieve those objectives and increase customer satisfaction. Ultimately, the successful CPO's efforts will advance the organization's business goals and promote its success.

In theory the CPO's job lies outside the technology realm, but in practice the CPO will necessarily collaborate with the CIO to provide the right tools to monitor, measure, and ultimately optimize the various business processes. Ideally, the CIO, a technologist, relies on the CPO, a business process expert, to guide the selection of technology meant to streamline business processes for the purpose of achieving business goals. Given the capabilities of a chosen technology, the CPO may redesign the business process. If a technology does not improve a business process, whether by reducing costs, improving quality, streamlining execution, or increasing productivity, then the organization doesn't really need that technology.

The CPO should even apply his skills and insights to the IT process itself. From provisioning new systems to adding new users, IT processes should fall within the scope of the CPO. How long does it take to add a new employee to the network or a provider to the supply chain? How costly is it to upgrade an application to a new release or to configure a new application for maximum benefit? All this and more should be subject to the kind of optimization a CPO can provide.

That's why we recommend to our clients that they have someone who fulfills the role of the CPO. It is far easier to implement the right technology the right way for companies whose foremost consideration is maintaining business processes that support their goals and objectives. This is especially true when it comes to business software—the software and the process must fit together in lockstep. Maybe we should have another rule of consulting economics for this, but we think the Second Rule covers it well enough. Just remember: *A successful business process trumps cool technology every time.* Companies that understand that can begin to liberate themselves from the IT business, and go back to focusing on business processes, strategies, and goals.

9
New Business Models

If we are going to liberate companies from being in the IT business—from software development, maintaining huge, complicated application infrastructures, from long learning curves, and costly IT support—we need an alternative. Companies need on-demand access to the capabilities of sophisticated systems and applications. They need software functionality that changes quickly and easily when their business changes. And they shouldn't have to assume the overhead of the entire IT infrastructure, enter into software development, or transform themselves into IT companies to get what they need. To that end, in the next two chapters, we'll introduce two new business models: Software-as-a-Service (SaaS), and the Managed Staffing model.

The SaaS Revolution

In early 2001, a year into business, Bluewolf caught the break we were looking for. Our first year had been successful, no doubt. We were paying ourselves, and had a growing customer list. We weren't about to turn back, but we understood the company was still in its infancy, and we were looking for ways to invent and define our future. We were also trying to figure out how best to serve our clients, who were still digging themselves out of the internet-bust rubble. And, looming ahead, unbeknownst to us all, was 9/11.

It was probably exactly a year after we made that trip to Olympus, that we attended a seminar in New York City hosted by a company called Salesforce.com. There were eight people in attendance. Salesforce's brilliant CEO, Marc Benioff, was one of them, carrying on with the same bravado that he now displays in front of thousands of people at his annual user conference.

We knew Marc. Eric worked with him 10 years earlier at Oracle, and when he saw us approach, he embraced us in a bear hug.

The story of Salesforce.com is well documented, but let it be said that they have managed to combine two ingredients that are transforming the software industry and finally making it safe for executives to hang their hopes on software initiatives:

1. **They built a hosted, multi-tenant operating system that delivers unprecedented economies of scale for BOTH themselves and their customers. There is a perfect alignment between vendor success and client success.**

2. **They created a culture and belief system within their company that to this day is unstoppable; the notion of clients that don't realize success is unheard of.**

Through it all, Salesforce.com has been a pioneering leader in the Software as a Service (SaaS) revolution, and as we have helped hundreds of their clients, we have grown to realize that SaaS—while still very young—is truly the answer to the software problem. Most importantly, for Bluewolf, it is the missing link that makes Agile an unstoppable approach to deploying applications.

SaaS promises to be the key to liberating most organizations from having to be in the IT business, and it ends the software nightmare that drove business managers crazy and made the big consulting firms rich. SaaS is the latest iteration of an old IT concept called time-sharing, but this time around the industry finally has it right, and the results are nothing short of revolutionary.

Time-sharing allowed multiple users to employ costly, complex software without investing in the IT infrastructure to run that software. It essentially spread the expense of the costly mainframe resource across many companies. For example, several timesharing companies would use the same core financial application. Users sat at dumb terminals, and could input data in highly structured ways the mainframe could handle. They could even generate a few canned reports. Companies using software on a timesharing basis paid only for the amount of the mainframe resource they used, which was usually a small fraction of the machine's capabilities. At a time when even small mainframes cost millions of dollars, and costly CPU time was billed out in nanosecond units, time-sharing allowed many companies to get the rudimentary benefits of computer automation at a price they could afford.

There were drawbacks to time-sharing, of course. Applications were delivered in one way only. User "choice" was restricted, for instance, to three different reports that could be formatted in four different ways. Custom reports–if they were even available—cost a fortune to code and took weeks to deliver. Time-sharing was, for all practical purposes, a one-size-fits-all model. It brings to mind Henry Ford's quip about his Model-T's, "You can have any color you want, as long as it's black." Beyond the lack of flexibility, screen navigation was cumbersome, and usage was anything but intuitive. Finally, the dumb terminals were just that—they couldn't be used for anything else other than to work with the mainframe.

With the introduction of PCs and the networking of most businesses, time-sharing evolved. Application service providers (ASPs), ran large servers at a central location, and hosted popular applications. However, software licensing requirements and constraints such as single tenancy required ASP customers to own their own copies of the application. That meant there was less to be gained in terms of economies of scale.

Things might have worked reasonably well for the client but many ASPs lost money hand over fist because the cost model did not work for them. This time the misalignment hurt the vendor, not the customer, but it still failed. Customer and vendor alignment is key in any complex software situation, and the fate of technology customers is closely wedded to that of their vendors. The business model has to work for both parties.

The ASP model, as we knew it then, had a number of problems. Customization remained costly and was discouraged, although the graphical PC interface offered an improvement in terms of ease of use. Mainly, all the arrangement saved the ASP customer was the expense of setting up a server, and the trouble of loading the application on it. In the end, there was little economic or operational advantage to the ASP model. After great fanfare, most ASPs went out of business. (Infrastructure providers, called Managed Service Providers, or MSPs, provided various infrastructure services like remote backup, and have proven more successful.)

Then came the Internet, the Web, the browser, Web services, dynamic technologies like Ajax, and SOA. SaaS evolved from these. Unlike timesharing, SaaS applications used the Web browser as the interface, which contributed to ease of use—virtually everybody knows how to use a Web browser. Unlike the ASP model, SaaS provides multi-tenancy. That means different users can use a single application simultaneously in different ways, without having to separately license the application. Furthermore, the SaaS application can be configured differently for each customer, and data can be securely stored and shielded from other customers. The economies of scale from shared tenancy made for low application pricing. Furthermore, SaaS applications were priced on a predictable annual subscription basis. Companies knew how much the application functionality would cost them each year; it was affordable, and they could budget for it.

SaaS effectively puts an end to the business software nightmare we described earlier in the book. It takes companies out of the software development business altogether. The software works as promised immediately, and has already been proven by other users. Since SaaS applications are highly configurable, that pretty much ends the customization headache. A SaaS customer can easily configure and reconfigure the application as often as desired. Good SaaS vendors continuously improve and enhance the software. These enhancements are folded right into the product automatically, often without the user even noticing. Gone are the days of painful transitions that accompanied software upgrades.

Salesforce.com, with its sales force automation/CRM functionality, quickly became the star of the SaaS model, and well-entrenched, long-established competitors like Siebel Systems just about vanished overnight in its wake. Today there are hundreds of SaaS business applications available covering the entire gamut of business functionality, including vertical industry applications.

Initially there were concerns about whether the SaaS model could scale to meet the needs of big businesses. Those concerns no longer exist; large companies as varied as Cisco, Nokia, Avis, AMD, and SunTrust are SaaS converts. Another concern focused on the issue of customization. That too has been resolved. At Bluewolf Group, we have been customizing client Salesforce implementations for years.

SaaS allows businesses of all sizes to quickly deploy state-of-the-art software functionality, configured for their specific use. From day one, a company can derive business value from running SaaS applications; within a few weeks, all of it's employees can be adept at its use. If the company changes its processes, it simply reconfigures the software quickly and easily with a few clicks of the mouse. No programmers are required, and the idea that change is a crisis disappears.

SaaS users don't have to install or maintain hardware beyond their existing network and browser-equipped desktops. The IT infrastructure requirements are minimal. In effect, SaaS takes companies out of the IT business, so they can focus on getting value from the software, not on making it work. The software works from the get-go, and functionality and cost are transparent. SaaS vendors typically roll out enhancements every 30 days without the customer needing to lift a finger. The user logs on and the new feature is there. Or, if there is a regulatory change, it is incorporated on the customer's behalf, without any work on their part. It really is that simple.

We were building our consulting firm following the business meltdown of 2000 to 2002. It didn't take us long to realize that SaaS was exactly what customers needed. It put an end to the costly, bloated applications that took forever to build and equally long to change. With SaaS, we realized that we could deliver specific business value to the customer in 30 days and guarantee it. So we did.

10

The End of HR: A New Staffing Model

Salesforce's Marc Benioff has crusaded for an "end to software." As he related to San Francisco Chronicle *writers in a 2006 interview, what he really means is the end to "the software model...the business and technology model that has dominated the industry for the last 25 to 30 years." He'd love to see companies move completely to SaaS. And while we're huge proponents of that vision, we also believe that, realistically, the SaaS revolution will take time. After all, almost 30 years after its inception, Oracle is still fighting to get the mainframe out of its customer's datacenters. We don't think the widespread embrace of, and transition to, Saas will take as long, given its tendency to deliver results, but we do think patience is in order.*

And, while that happens, clients still need lots of help with the old stuff, by which we mean virtually every enterprise client server application sold over the past twenty years. Finding that help has become increasingly difficult for organizations, who are stuck between a world of outsourcing or offshoring. Many feel their choices are limited—companies can hand over their datacenter to IBM, or they can go cut a deal with offshoring giants Infosys or Tata, (though the latter option is only viable for those entering into multi-million dollar deals).

And CIOs today, stuck between these two industry trends, are thirsty for the one thing they can't find in the U.S.: skilled workers, brought into the organization by HR. But just as the old model of application development didn't provide the functionality companies needed fast enough to meet their changing business needs, so too the costly, cumbersome, traditional approach to staffing can't get them the skills they need today and the different skills they may need tomorrow

Companies need a new staffing model—one that is project-based. Now, we're not talking about the sort of IT projects we were so down on several chapters back. By project-based staffing, we mean initiatives intended to address specific business issues and deliver specific business results. Forrester Research, in fact, launched a new research service focused on project-based businesses, which tells us that the project-based approach to business is spreading widely.

Our vision of the new HR staffing model has five main components: project-based staffing, remote staffing, outsourced tasking, temporary use of specialists, and empowered staff.

Project-based staffing

People are deployed on a project basis in order to deliver specific business value. Projects can be of short or long duration, or ongoing. The key is that they have a specific focus, and they are somehow tied to specific business value.

Empowered staff

For projects to succeed, the staff needs to fully understand the project and its business goals, and must be empowered to make the decisions that will enable it to achieve those goals. Once a company assembles a talented staff and equips them with the knowledge they need, it must trust them do their jobs and make the right decisions.

Temporary use of specialists

Sometimes companies need specialists onsite for a given project, but don't have enough of a need to justify hiring top-notch talent permanently. In that case, the specialists can parachute in for a few days, weeks, or months to perform the task.

Remote staffing

Given the ubiquitous presence of the Internet, new communications strides, and available collaborative tools, staffers can be located anywhere. A DBA residing in Omaha, for example, can meet your needs for the management of data residing in New York City, Florida, or Texas.

Outsourced tasking

This is related to remote staffing, but differs in that the person working remotely need not be on a company's payroll at all. This is especially useful for those that need highly specialized skills on a project, but can't justify hiring a topnotch expert. Outsourcing that particular task essentially amounts to "renting" a top-notch expert with the necessary expertise. When that can be done remotely, so much the better.

Of course, companies contending with staffing issues and new employment models must deal with the issue of outsourcing. The 21st century is the era of the global economy, and outsourcing, which we'll talk about at length in the next chapter, will be a permanent fact of life. As we discuss in the "Bluewolf White Paper on Offshore Outsourcing," the fact that many companies have chosen to move IT jobs overseas en masse has understandably drawn considerable ire from US programmers, systems administrators, and computer engineers. Unemployment rates among stateside IT professionals rose steadily between 2000 and 2004, and this was occurring in a field previously known for high employment rates and job security. According to the US Department of Labor's Bureau of Labor Statistics, outsourcing is a key factor in the increasingly limited nature of job opportunities for stateside computer programmers. As the Bureau noted at the time: "Programmers are at a much higher risk of having their jobs outsourced abroad than are workers involved in more complex and sophisticated information technology functions, such as software engineering, because computer programming has become an international language, requiring little localized or specialized knowledge. Additionally, the work of computer programmers can be routinized, once knowledge of a particular programming language is mastered."

Stateside programmers may face another job security challenge as technologies like SaaS take on greater importance to business enterprises. Programmers will still have a role to play, but businesses will have a far greater need for IT-savvy business and process analysts who possess the skills to help their clients or their own companies get the most of out technologies like SaaS.

11

The Realities of Outsourcing

The global economy is a fact of life, and there isn't a business today that isn't affected by it in some way. Even if you think your business isn't a player in the global economy, you can bet your suppliers are. Outsourcing, especially offshore outsourcing, is just another manifestation of the global economy.

Few industries have embraced or been impacted by globalization as much as the information technology sector. The global technology boom and the potential for business growth and development in foreign countries—despite (or perhaps because of) the burst of the Internet bubble and a flagging stateside economy post-9/11—made the climate ripe for globalization. Instantaneous information transfer in the form of the Internet and the World Wide Web, combined with the theoretical bridging effect of common software languages and the promise of cheap, skilled IT labor, have driven the offshore outsourcing trend.

Mirroring the way companies deal with the globalization of IT is the incongruous way that they approach IT internally. On the one hand, they pay lip service to the idea of IT as a strategic differentiator. They understand that as the critical enabler of new revenue-producing products and services, IT can help organizations gain a competitive advantage over their rivals. We've all heard the classic examples of IT as a strategic differentiator: Wal-Mart uses information to squeeze every penny out of the supply and distribution chain, thereby undercutting their competitors on price. FedEx used its package tracking to differentiate itself from bigger rivals, though many have since caught up. Google used its IT ability in the form of matching advertising with search content to pull ahead of a pack of formidable competitors, including Microsoft and Yahoo.

When IT is a competitive differentiator, it pays to invest top dollar, because it will bring the kind of high return on investment (ROI) companies seek. This return can take the form of increased revenue, reduced costs, greater customer satisfaction and loyalty, entrée into totally new markets, and more.

But many of the same companies that call IT a strategic differentiator also view IT as a cost center to be minimized. Lots of managers believe that IT doesn't give them any competitive advantage. Rather, they feel they have to have it because customers and other stakeholders expect it. They are satisfied if staff has a minimum level of IT competence. Their approach is to spend the least amount of money on IT that they can get away with. When such companies encounter financial difficulties, IT is the first thing to get cut.

If you have read this book up to this point, then you know we are the last to encourage managers to spend big bucks on IT, except when absolutely necessary. And even then, we believe there are smart ways to get strategic advantage from IT without spending the huge sums that have historically been required.

The tricky thing about outsourcing, especially offshore outsourcing, is that it plays to both sides of this debate. It can enable IT as a strategic differentiator and it can allow managers to minimize their IT expenses. In some cases it can do both at the same time. But sometimes it doesn't help companies save money at all—and may even be costly. To figure out what it might do for your company, you need to separate the facts from the myths of outsourcing.

The first myth is that outsourcing saves significant amounts of money. The reality is that companies must make significant upfront investments in outsourcing or offshoring, and even then they will not see immediate cost savings. Simply comparing the salary of an overseas worker with a US worker, and calculating the cost savings based on that, is simplistic and potentially dangerous.

The fact is that there are significant costs to outsourcing (some of which we summarized in earlier chapters). Don't mistake the ease and speed with which you can transfer information to offshore workers, or get their results back from the offshore outsourcing provider, with automatic cost savings. Like any relationship, it takes time and effort to build a viable and effective outsourcing relationship with an offshore IT provider. Realistically, we believe this will be at least a yearlong undertaking. And time, as that old business truism goes, is money.

Before companies can expect that any work exported to overseas coders or call centers will be delivered with results comparable to what they get at home, they have to spend considerable time communicating with the outsourcing provider. This represents a considerable financial investment. Serious attention must be paid to searching for a firm that can truly meet the needs of the company. The expenses involved in vendor selection alone can be quite significant: there's travel, training, visa sponsorship for offshore workers learning systems stateside, protecting intellectual property, ensuring the privacy of customer data, working out all the myriad contractual details, and more.

Another myth is that—at least when it comes to IT—we live in one unified world. That may sound good in a Coke commercial (Hey, *we'd* like to teach the world to sing in perfect harmony), but the reality is far different. Even though offshore providers speak English and program in the same universal computer languages we use (C, C++, Java, Javascript, XML, etc.) significant cultural differences can present formidable challenges that must be recognized and addressed. What overseas coders might regard as an intuitive interface may be utterly confusing to users here. Customers may not be able to understand the spoken accents of overseas call center representatives even though they scored perfectly on written English exams. Only companies that really invest the time to understand the myriad cultural factors that impact an offshoring arrangement can make the setup work. That means devoting time to face-to-face interaction with the offshore vendor, and *that* brings us to travel.

Does anyone think the travel expenses entailed in outsourcing are low? Bits and bytes might travel over the Internet for free and nearly instantaneously, but people don't. To achieve the kind of communications and understanding necessary for successful projects, you will have to invest not only in traveling overseas regularly, but also in bringing the overseas folks here. Remember that time spent in a foreign country is time not spent on work here. And you can't jump over to a meeting in Mumbai as easily as you go from New York to Washington. Offshore outsourcing involves tiring, draining travel for which you pay a price not only in airfares and hotels, but in lost productivity and managerial and staff fatigue.

Another myth is that the Internet is free. Yes, the Internet enables offshoring, and it is a sunk expense that doesn't cost more after the initial investment, up to a point. The fact, however, is that the IT infrastructure is critical. At the least, companies have to plan on major spending for big communications pipes, which aren't cheap. We haven't priced out a T1 link to India or China lately, but we certainly wouldn't want to assume that we'd be happy to pay for it month after month.

Okay, let's say you've thought through all the offshore outsourcing issues and decided that it is worth it. You still have to figure out which specific IT work you should send offshore. Now the type of work becomes key. Can you send call centers overseas? Probably, but be aware that customers may complain if they have problems understanding the call center representatives' accents (or, for that matter, if the reps have trouble understanding *them*). How about basic coding? Sure, this is done often, and with some success. Should mission critical operations go overseas? That depends on your organization's tolerance for risk, and how well you want to sleep at night. Then there is the question of project duration. Long haul development might be ripe for offshoring, but projects meant to last under a year probably don't make sense. You'll hardly have time to get acquainted with the vendor. Heck, you'll barely have recovered from jet lag (remember, we're talking 12 to 18 hour flights).

Then, there are the political implications of offshoring. Whatever your domestic workers think about the issue, offshoring IT won't exactly send them reassuring signals about the company or their positions in it. Whatever justification management offers will be considered self-serving bull. Count on it. Unionized workers may be up in arms, and they could organize action. Between restructuring costs and productivity losses due to demoralized workers, your bottom line could take a significant hit.

Perhaps the biggest mistake a company can make when it comes to offshore outsourcing is to assume that once it has selected a vendor, it can simply shift work overseas, get its order filled, and carry on with whatever it's doing at home, only with less—if any—domestic IT support. Successful offshoring requires that the company develop and maintain an ongoing relationship with the vendor, so only those companies in it for the long haul, with the intent to maintain a vested overseas presence, are likely to save any money and come out ahead. Although the initial investment will be high—especially in terms of development and relationship management—over time, those companies may realize real cost savings.

In fact, cost savings, which most managers cite as the primary reason for offshore outsourcing, may not be the best reason. Rather, the ability to work around the clock by taking advantage of the time zone differences (offshore providers code while stateside workers sleep, and vice versa), to speed time to market, or to increase quality may be.

The domestic political debate over immigration is one other aspect of offshoring that merits discussion. This is as divisive an issue as it gets. U.S. Senators Dick Durbin (D-IL) and Chuck Grassley (R-IA) introduced The H-1B and L-1 Visa Fraud and Abuse Prevention Act of 2007 at the end of March 2007. The stated purpose was to overhaul the H-1B and L-1 visa programs to give priority to American workers, and to crack down on unscrupulous employers who deprive qualified Americans of high-skill jobs. Don't expect the issue go away anytime soon. Already, the immigration debate is shaping up to be a hot topic in the 2008 presidential election.

There has been an ongoing battle related to these visa programs, as different interests push for higher or lower quotas. Where companies stand on the issue reflects their need for skilled labor, how cheaply they want to get it, and at what social cost. In the end, it is just another example of how supply and demand plays out in a dynamic, free marketplace. Stateside, fewer people are going into—or staying in—IT, and a significant factor in that drop-off relates to job insecurity due to offshoring. Conversely, the IT boom overseas means more people there are electing to go into the field. Meanwhile those who are most talented are most in demand, and can choose where to work. Turnover, whether stateside or overseas, is increasing.

Of course, one problem with trying to pinpoint the situation in IT employment is its fluidity. In the April 2007 issue of *InformationWeek*, writer Marianne Kolbasuk McGee cited an average 2.3% IT unemployment based on Bureau of Labor Statistics figures. That means that for all practical purposes, there is no IT unemployment. The figure for non-IT professional jobs was 2.2%. So, despite the growth of offshoring, IT workers in the U.S. are finding employment, at least based on the macro statistics. Anecdotally, we are hearing many of our clients complain about how hard it is to find qualified IT people.

Therefore, computer software engineers and computer scientists—particularly those who stay current with and maintain competency in emerging technologies—have as good or better prospects for US employment than ever before. Companies for whom overseas outsourcing makes sense still should consider cross-training internal employees in more advanced functions. The payback in morale, smooth transition, company image to shareholders, and such may be worth the investment. Forward-looking companies must recognize that shorter-term gains realized by farming out IT projects shouldn't trump long-term competitiveness and creative momentum in their fields. IT is indeed a global industry, and one that can deliver significant IT advantage. US companies risk being outpaced by rising contenders in the international IT field if they cease to cultivate homegrown talent. With the expansion of IT within individual businesses, various industries, and in the US and globally, companies are going to need all the IT skills they can get if they want to compete in the 21st century.

So, why are we talking about outsourcing and offshoring in a book about agile consulting? The answer is simple: we think that agile consulting as we practice it can reduce your need to look offshore for lower IT costs, or to get IT that provides a strategic differentiator. Through agile consulting practices, we can help you do it with your own people and augment them where needed.

How will this work for IT in the future? In the next chapter we look briefly at the IT organization on the horizon, and share what we expect to see 5 to 10 years from now.

12

The 21ˢᵗ Century IT Department

We can say two things with great certainty about the IT department of the future: It will be considerably smaller—perhaps one-third of its current size—and it will have a much greater business process focus. The geeks and techies who thrived deep within the IT department will be a lot lonelier in the future, because companies will staff far fewer than before. The entire IT department will be much more focused on and better aligned with the actual business of the organization. Organizations for the most part will be liberated from being in the business of IT.

That certainly isn't the case now. Large and even midsize organizations find themselves trying to replicate the IT infrastructure and capabilities of a professional software development organization or of a computer products company, as if they were a mini-Microsoft, or a junior Oracle. All the while, their actual business may be making and marketing shoes, or distributing industrial supplies, or providing logistical services, or any of zillions of other business endeavors that *aren't* actually IT.

Many companies' internal IT organizations were started sometime during the end of the previous century (in the 1980s and 1990s, and sometimes earlier) and today, look like scaled-down (or not so scaled-down) versions of software companies. They have teams of software developers, teams to handle software quality assurance and testing, and teams to handle user interface development and application design. They employ others to try to integrate all the pieces together, and employ even more people just to operate and maintain the department.

All the skills required for performing these tasks needed to reside in-house. That meant companies had to find, hire, train, and retain skilled, qualified IT staff. That is not a trivial undertaking, to say the least. Then they had to do all the things a good business does, like provide all of these people with a career path, with the ability to gain certifications, and the opportunity to attend professional development conferences. That's nice, except for one small problem: IT wasn't their business. It was simply something these companies thought they had to have to run their business. But IT people are expensive; having them on staff represents a huge cost.

And the costs didn't stop with the people, although that was the largest part of it. Companies also had to buy numerous software development, testing, and management tools. You can't install a professional caliber IT shop and not provide the same kind of tools IT professionals use at the big software companies. So whether they intended to be or not, once companies added the cost of the tools, workstations, and other infrastructure on top of the people costs, they were suddenly in the IT business big time. Worse, IT sucked up capital resources that would have been better spent by businesses to enhance their core competencies.

The organizational chart on the following page draws the picture better than anything we can describe.

IT Organization Today

($3 billion company)

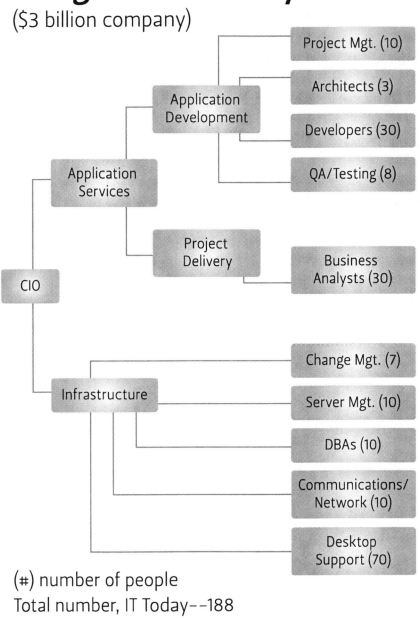

(#) number of people
Total number, IT Today--188

This diagram depicts an organization we met with in 2007. The company supports 188 people in IT. Sure, it is a big company, but 188 extra mouths to feed has to impact its bottom line. Remember, these aren't cheap mouths to feed, either.

It's not that we have anything against IT. We both come from IT backgrounds. We love IT. We just don't love it *as* IT. We love it for what it can do for the business and business processes. The people who really want the heavy tech jobs need to go to work for technology companies or technology service providers. Our remote DBA service employs lots of DBAs so our clients don't have to. It's nothing personal—we love DBAs, and coders, and testers, and people who do all sorts of other IT functions; we just don't think those positions belong in the org charts of most of our clients. (To get our take on IT hiring and salary trends check out the Appendix: IT Salary Guide, at the end of this book.)

So what skills will the new in-house IT group hire? You can tell from the previous chart. They will need lots of business process analysts, business process designers, and business analysts. They will need project managers, and trainers to drive adoption. And then, they will need to let Salesforce.com, SaaS vendors, Microsoft, Oracle, or SAP hire the hard core IT people.

Now that we have described the 21st century IT department, let's meet the 21st century consultant.

13
The 21st Century Consultant

The consultants we hire today—what we think of as 21st century consultants—are very different from those who came into consulting as recently as the late 1990s, before bloated ERP thankfully fell out of favor, and before the dotcom bust. To begin with, they are stepping into a completely different consulting culture.

The consolidation within the elite ranks of consulting firms, in which the so-called Big 8 shrunk to the Big 6, then to the Big 4, to what now may be the Big 2, has begun to tarnish the appeal of working for a consulting firm. That's a big change from the consulting climate in the late 1990s. Articles is accounting industry journals in the late 1990s cited surveys showing that management consulting had become the top career choice for the MBA crowd of business school graduates. Articles in other magazines at that time noted that entry-level positions in consulting firms were not only safe jobs to accept from a career advancement standpoint, but that partnership was increasingly the preferred career objective.

Just a few years after those articles appeared, Christopher McKenna wrote in *The World's Newest Profession: Management Consulting in the*

Twentieth Century, that "the economic downturn in 2000 had left most of the business school students scrambling to find jobs." Certainly the elite management consulting firms—McKinsey, Booz Allen Hamilton, Bain, etc.—remained a preferred career path for the non-entrepreneurial best and brightest coming out of the top business schools. But beyond those highly selective firms, the market had dramatically changed.

The graduates of the 1997 MBA schools were intent on joining consulting firms, thanks to the promise of long term employment, prestige, travel (which was often appealing to young grads), and high pay—including equity or stock options which, back in 1997, stood a good chance of developing into significant capital. (It is interesting to note, however, that as of this writing there has not been a single, notable, IPO for a consulting firm since 2000.) The goal was to get in the door, get onto a client engagement, and milk it for everything it was worth in an effort to build the firm's billings. This was the proven way to pave a career path to partnership.

The firms desperately needed these fat, open-ended consulting engagements to support their growing ranks of partners. They needed the marathon requirements development phases and the lifetime software implementation annuities to generate the revenue required to support those partners. They needed armies of rank-and-file consultants at the base level to support the uppermost layers of the consulting pyramid. And their model worked, because while the minions were sitting in conference rooms billing $300 an hour, the partners were taking the executives that owned those conference rooms to play golf, to lavish dinners, or even to gentlemen's clubs, ensuring that as the project deadlines slipped and the budgets soared, the executives would still support their efforts.

The Enron debacle and similar corporate disasters tarnished the entire elite accounting/consulting firm class, and forced the firms to separate their accounting practices from their consulting practices. Then, a funny thing started to happen. Partnership in these types of firms, a number of consultants realized, might not be such a great thing if it meant being called before investigators or a judge and jury to answer uncomfortable questions about ones' role in what had been going on with an unscrupulous client. The Sarbanes-Oxley Act of 2002 only reinforced these growing concerns by mandating what amounted to the documentation of accountability at the highest management levels. The consulting firms, already reeling from the economic downturn, now found themselves being scrutinized as never before. And a lot of people didn't like the feel of the heat.

In the meantime, the rank-and-file consultants not only learned the customer's business so they could advise them, but they went even farther. Actually, we think they went too far by "going native," and becoming an actual part of their customer's culture. They began to think like their customer and adopt their customer's worldview, jargon, and value system. They might retain whatever lingering cachet the consulting firm mantle bestowed, but they had become, for all practical purposes, one and the same with their customers. And lots of them actually took it over the brink by accepting full-time jobs with their clients. They had "gone back to industry," as those in the consulting business call it.

In effect, these armies of consultants got totally enmeshed in their client's culture, despite the fact that—along with their newly minted MBAs and analytical skills—they were initially hired to bring fresh ideas and an outside perspective to the company. Of course, clients want their consultants to understand their business dynamics and their specific processes, but what they really need is for the consultants to bring new knowledge they don't have in-house. They need the perspective that allows the consultant to see things the company may have overlooked. Maybe a sacred company cow is blocking the view of the problem and its solution. People inside the company are usually too close to the problem to see it. But the outside consultant is supposed to have the perspective to see beyond, around, or through these sacred cows.

By going native, however, the consultants sacrificed their independent, fresh perspectives. They quickly became blinded in the same ways as everyone else in the company. By drinking exclusively from the same well as their customers, they lost any source of inspiration for new ideas, and they learned to play the same political games that already haunted the caverns of the company. They became corporate policy and process wonks, cranking out the same old poison as everyone else—even if they were putting it in new bottles. As we said above, over time many consultants go so far native they actually end up being hired by their customers—the ultimate sign that they failed to consult. So much for them doing the job of the independent consultant.

Traditional consulting firms, born out of the 20th century, seemed right at home with Thomas Carlyle's Great Man theory. Mainstream society no longer embraced the Victorian Scottish historian's assertion that "The history of the world is but the biography of great men," but consulting firms banked their success on its validity. We also call this our "Wizard of Oz" theory. In most big consulting firms, the path to completion on many projects amounted to a long, windy, shiny, yellow brick road. At the end of that road, was the wizard—the Great Man—who could deliver the project to the Promised Land. The good consulting firms were masters at delaying the arrival of this man—or bringing him in occasionally to temper client angst, before rushing him out to the next client—all the while keeping the project status reports from showing red, danger.

This man might be a partner, or a super-charged project manager, or an MIT engineer who could unwind a jumble of poorly written software code. Whoever he was, the weight of the world typically lay on his shoulders to accomplish what no other person could. *That* is a recipe for disaster. Rarely, if ever, can a complex software project be driven or rescued by a single individual. In fact, rarely in life do we come across single individuals that can pull off feats as complex and multi-faceted as a software project—even in the SaaS world, where the software is pre-installed and most of the work is business process-oriented.

Business projects, and software projects, are team sports. Period. And if you think about team sports in general, the Great Man theory falls on its face. In the history of basketball, for example, there are perhaps a handful of examples of individuals who actually carried their teams to success—Michael Jordan, Wilt Chamberlain, Bill Russell, and Larry Bird come to mind. Basketball fans would argue that even these men were supported by great teams. Even if, for the sake of argument, we call them Great Men, it's undeniable that most of the great accomplishments in basketball were the result of extraordinary efforts exerted by teams, and most of these accomplishments cannot be captured statistically in the box scores. The 2005 Detroit Pistons were an unheralded group of players that dominated the NBA playoffs and finals. They did not have a Kobe Bryant or a Shaquille O'Neal. They won games because they worked together, they created together, and probably debated together behind closed doors over a long season, but they ultimately got the task done as a collective group of driven individuals.

Enterprise software projects are no different. Are you going to bank the success of your next project on finding a Great Man? Or are you better off embracing a team-based approach to success? You can probably guess where we stand on this one, but there's no denying that the idea of the Great Man remains irresistible to many. It's simply a more romantic notion that a single great achiever can outshine and outperform everyone else. Take for example, Accenture's ad campaign featuring Tiger Woods. The ads liken top companies' attributes—including Accenture's own—to Tiger's; newer ads feature the slogan "We know what it takes to be a Tiger." Though they don't explicitly suggest that a single person is responsible for their own success or that of the companies they serve, Accenture nonetheless implies that—at least in the golfing world—the Great Man exists. (In our view, it's a moot point—we don 't see that Tiger's powerful drive off the tee has to anything do with Accenture's ability to make an SAP project work right.)

In any case, we feel the Great Man concept is inherently flawed. Even if such people exist, the idea places utterly unrealistic burdens upon them. Kent Beck understood this when he developed XP, and ensured it was something that any programmer could work with. XP doesn't need genius programmers. Well, something similar can be said of agile consulting as we envision it. Agile consulting can be undertaken by ordinary mortals. It doesn't require a Great Man to pull everything together and save us from going over a cliff. So let's make this the Ninth Law of Consulting Economics: *Do not rely on the Great Man for project salvation.*

That is not to say that we don't call in process or technical experts, or bring in specialists at various points. Of course we do. But the success of a project, and its ability to deliver business value never rests on the shoulders of one individual, no matter how great he or she may be.

So who is this 21ˢᵗ century consultant? He or she is an agile consultant steeped in the concepts of agile and iterative development, XP, and agile consulting, and works side by side with the client as a partner and independent advisor.

In Agile project management, the concept of an all-powerful project manager does not exist either. Agile projects consist of self-organizing teams, and the ideas and the direction of the project are debated and decided on by the team—not the project manager. The project manager's main responsibility is to manage the Product Backlog, which is essentially a list of features and functionality that remain to be delivered.

The consultant of the 21st century never goes native. He doesn't expect to work with a client long enough to do so. And, more importantly, the Agile consultant of the 21st century CAN'T go native. She could not survive, and has no desire to try to, in the very corporate culture for which she is consulting. That would be akin to a marriage counselor moving in with the family. The agile consultant of the 21st century may have spent time in industry, and he or she certainly needs to have battled it out in the corporate trenches, but the successful consultants of this century thrive and provide value because they are different, and almost incapable of going native.

The agile consultants of the 21st century are not beholden to the client. They are beholden to their team, and to other consultants from their firm or their own network with whom they collaborate. This is extremely valuable to the client, because the minute the consultant becomes beholden to the client, they *are* native, and their value is lost. They begin to agree with company policy for the sake of politics and longevity, as opposed to disagreeing for the sake of value. By contrast, the 21st Century Agile Consultant intends to complete the current project in a matter of a few weeks. His mission is to look at the client's business and processes from the vantage point of a knowledgeable outsider.

As importantly, this new breed of consultant is part of a small, self-directed team of similarly independent individuals. The team brings in people with specialized expertise or skills where and when it needs them. Every member of the team is important, yet ultimately replaceable. There is no Great Man or Great Woman anywhere in sight.

This new breed of consultant communicates with the team and the client regularly. He or she knows that insights, understanding, and results come through dialogue and the lively, frequent exchange of ideas. Agile consulting adopts the concept of dialogue from agile development methodologies like Scrum. As Craig Larman explains in *Agile & Iterative Development: A Manager's Guide,* Scrum calls for self-organizing teams, and features daily team measurement. A hallmark of Scrum is the daily stand-up meeting, or Scrum meeting, at which the same set of questions is asked of every person on the team. Look at the Scrum questions in the side box, and you will notice that everything about the Scrum meeting drives toward one thing—keeping the team focused on producing the current iteration within the specified timebox.

As importantly, the 21ˢᵗ consultant is driven to make the client self-sufficient. Just as a contractor builds a house that someone else will be able to comfortably inhabit, the Agile consultant makes sure that when she delivers a project, the client can take over the application—or even the next phase of the project—on his own. Creating this self-sufficiency does not mean that the consultant's sole responsibility is to leave behind documentation. It is rare that documentation is sufficiently complete, or that it can be picked up—and actually understood—by another individual. The devilish details left out in documentation are always the details that matter. That is no one's fault—it is just the reality of trying to do something really complex.

So, the Agile consultant of the 21ˢᵗ century is a mentor, a teacher, and, most importantly, a communicator. This individual is an expert at involving the client in the entire process, and making them feel a part of it. The consultant lets clients put their hands on the steering wheel, and shows them how to drive the success of a project, and how to manage the system that is being deployed.

Scrum Questions

What have you done since the last Scrum?

What will you do between now and the next Scrum (tomorrow)?

What is getting in the way of meeting the iteration goals?

Are we missing any tasks?

Have you learned or decided anything new, of relevance to some of the team members?

(source: Larman, pg. 121)

As consultants rather than developers, our questions and discussions may be a little different from the Scrum questions in the box, but the goal is the same: To keep the team focused on the latest iteration, and to make sure we are delivering the business value that the customer wants. We also keep the customer fully in the communication loop, which leads to another aspect of our style of 21st century consultancy—full disclosure.

Full disclosure means providing complete project transparency. The team and the client know all the details of the project, including goals, schedule, results to date, setbacks, and problems; in short, everything that affects the project is disclosed. Compare that to the typical experience with a big conventional consulting firm. Projects would disappear from the client's sight for weeks or months at a time. They'd never know who was actually doing what, or when they were doing it. Their only point of contact was, typically, a low-level account manager and maybe a monthly meeting. Only clients that pushed might get a hint that a problem had been encountered or a milestone had been delayed. Forget about hearing the details—unless it was time for the consulting firm to start making excuses. All this leads to our Tenth Law of Consulting Economics: *Full project transparency avoids surprises.*

What are some of the tenants of "full project transparency?" Here is a good list with which to start:

1. The human resources on a project are interviewed and hand picked by the client. There is no question about their background, prior experience, or capabilities.

2. The Success Criteria of a project is jointly crafted and agreed upon—in writing—by the client and consultant team.

3. The Product Backlog is agreed to and managed by the joint client/consultant team.

4. There is a daily, 15-minute, standing meeting that the client is invited to and SHOULD attend. The purpose of this meeting is to understand the tasks of the day and to identify any roadblocks that need attention.

5. The project plan, all project documentation, and a daily updated Executive Status dashboard is maintained and accessed in a central database.

6. The project budget is tracked in real time and is accessible by the entire joint client/consultant team.

7. There is a one-hour weekly status call where all project issues are discussed and recorded for the entire joint team.

8. There is a bi-weekly Executive Status call where the client and consultant executives are briefed on the project status and given an opportunity to make critical decisions.

9. Working software—or a working model—is delivered on a continual, rapid basis. All decisions regarding software functionality are made through the use of working models, as opposed to the use of detailed documentation.

The willingness to engage in healthy, constructive debate among the team, and especially with the client, is another characteristic of our new breed of consultant. We believe in listening to clients, and really hearing what they have to say. However, that doesn't mean we will necessarily agree. We don't drink the client's Kool-Aid. If something is wrong, we say it. We resolve disagreements through iterations. Rather than argue and debate, which wastes energy and time, we try new things until we know what works best. Conventional consultants have to try to get it perfectly right the first time because the cost of getting it wrong is astronomical. With agile consulting, we can try something; if it doesn't work we try something else. We don't have to get it perfect; we just want to get close, and then, with each quick iteration, closer and closer still. The cost of change is minimal.

Our new breed of consultant also is a consensus builder. Again, it quickly becomes obvious to team members and to the client what the right approach or decision should be, because we have iterations to work with right in front of us. Plus, the transparency we advocate makes it very clear that every project will involve tradeoffs—for example, getting one piece of complex functionality might result in something else getting cut, or it may enlarge a budget. These things are discussed and accentuated on a daily basis, making it easier over the long haul to come to a consensus. There is no need to rally around a Great Man who will pull everything together. Success becomes the team's success and the client's success. The only thing that counts is delivering the agreed upon results, and from that the team gets the credit. As it works out, there's never blame, because what might turn into a failure with a conventional approach is quickly corrected in the next iteration through agile consulting. We identify and fix problems before they lead to failures. Problems simply become jumping-off points for the next iteration in the pipeline. If it takes another rev of our engines to get there, that's a tiny price to pay.

It is probably important to mention at this point—if it hasn't been made clear already—that enterprise software consulting is a full-contact sport. By that, we mean that the successful consultant's primary objective is to deliver customer success. Many inexperienced consultants—and consultants who operate by the Great Man model—think that the primary objective in an engagement is to make friends with the client. And this very naiveté leads to many a failed project. To the contrary, the successful Agile consultant of the 21st Century needs to be confident enough to challenge and debate with their client while attempting to determine the optimal approach to customer success. And this requires an individual who has an extreme ability to do the following:

1.   Over–communicate.

This isn't as obvious as it may sound. The consultant who quietly assumes that everyone is on the same page, and who is afraid to repeat-

edly state the obvious (for example, "The goal of this project is to central-
ize customer data in a single, accessible database."), is the consultant who
will unknowingly lose the confidence of his customer and who will find
him or herself looking for new work.

2. Support the team.

There will be times in every project where the impulse to blame an
individual for a problem will overcome a consultant's rational notion to
support the team. The Agile consultant of the 21ˢᵗ century resists this
temptation. And while a project team's makeup may sometimes need to
be changed, those adjustments should never be construed as an opportunity to blame a single individual for a failure. It is the responsibility
of the team as a whole to ensure that no single individual is placed in a
position where personal missteps can derail an entire project. The irony is
that most seasoned CIOs understand the importance of architecting systems to ensure that there is no single point of failure. A football team has
multiple blockers, receivers, and backups at each position. Why should a
project team be any different?

3. Blow it up.

If the client is not providing the information, support, or user involvement necessary to pull off a successful engagement, then the consultant
needs to be willing to "blow it up," and sacrifice the short-term peace to
seek a better approach. Many projects in corporate America lack executive support, or the right level of involvement from the people who will
actually use the application, or derive value from its benefit. In these situations—and in others—the successful 21ˢᵗ century Agile consultant is not
afraid to call a spade a spade and elevate the issue. On paper, this sounds
easier than it is. In reality, blowing up a project issue takes skill, proper
communication, and confidence. And most times, it is a gut call that the
individual consultant initiates. It can't be merely reactionary. But when
done correctly, blowing up a project issue can sometimes be the course
correction that leads to a successful deployment.

This seems to be a natural point to talk about our own agile consulting methodology, which we think of as "Consulting for the 21st Century." Unlike the methodologies of the conventional consulting firms, our agile consulting methodology won't fill dozens of three-ring binders—or even one. It isn't a cookbook for consultants. Rather, it is a concise, three-step approach to software implementation with the goal of delivering business value fast. The key to our model is Time-to-Value.

Our approach can be summed up in three words that can be explained in half a page: Translate, Transform, Transcend. Let's look at each step a little more closely:

Translate

This is where we, working with the client, translate the client's business process into working models. Mainly, it involves pinning down the business process workflow, mapping requirements, and migrating data. If integration is required, this is where we identify it. The results of this step lay the foundations for a Success Plan that defines what the client will regard as success, a project plan that lays out how we will proceed, and working models—actual, live software that demonstrates areas of the application around which we need to build consensus. How does our Translate phase differ from the "Requirements Definition" phase of a traditional waterfall methodology? The answer is very simple. Even though we have translated requirements, and even though we have a pretty good idea of what we are building at the end of the Translate phase, nothing is set is stone. Things can still change. Requirements can still emerge. In fact, our Agile process encourages new requirements to emerge. In traditional waterfall methodologies, requirements get locked down. Things need to be defined 100% up front. From our perspective, in a dynamic business world where things change fast and where people don't necessarily read or completely understand a requirements specification, "locking down" requirements can be a dangerous thing.

Transform

This is the heavy lifting phase where we transform the working models into a live application. It involves setup and configuration of the production system, often a SaaS application, and whatever data migration and integration is required. Key to the Transform phase of an Agile project is ensuring that the future users of the application are involved in testing and providing feedback on the application. Typically, we will create a test group of 5 to 10 users who will be intimately engaged in the entire Transform process. They will provide feedback at a keyboard, and we will make changes to the application on the fly, ensuring that nothing is lost in translation. If a user tells us that something is right, that we have nailed it, after testing the application, then we know that we have it right. And that positive user feedback is the only thing that satisfies us.

Central also to the Transform phase is the execution of Change Management and User Adoption plans. These are critical. Many organizations assume that users will simply swallow new technology applications whole. They fail to realize that changing human behavior is the single most daunting task in any engagement. And deploying a new application demands that people change their behavior. That is often a difficult and risky prospect, because even if the change is a good one, and may be for the users' own benefit, people tend to resist it. Change Management involves the internal marketing of the new application to the user community. It strives to provide the emotional and psychological preparation for the change that is about to take place. In some cases, this may be as simple as having executive management send a series of emails to users extolling the benefits of the new application, and getting people prepared and excited for its arrival. In other cases, it may involve a graphically intense marketing campaign that involves posters, contests, and even promotional gimmicks. Whatever the case, it is extremely important that organizations prepare their users for the new application that is coming. It shouldn't be a mystery. It shouldn't just arrive. And whenever possible, the change should be supported by key individuals who are thought leaders within the organization. Nothing will doom a project more than poor acceptance from users. And nothing can lower the risk of project adoption more than preparing users up front.

At the end of the Transform phase, everything is ready to go. The application is built, the data is converted, the integration is in place, the training is ready to be delivered, and the users are excited to get started with it.

Transcend

One of the biggest mistakes organizations make when investing in software development or application deployment, is that they treat the project as if it is a point-in-time event. They budget for and put focus on the project as if it has a definitive start date and a definitive end date. And they assume that the resulting system—whether it is an in-house data warehouse or a SaaS-based CRM system—will exist on its own as a static asset.

Companies fail to realize that an enterprise software application is a living system. When it is first deployed, it is in its infancy, and like a child, the system will need to grow with the organization in order to deliver long-term value. In our third phase, the Transcend phase, we work with companies to ensure that their organization is prepared to enhance the application as quickly as the users demand.

The consequence of delivering a little bit of cool functionality to technology users is that it whets their appetite for more. And the speed with which newer and different functionality can be deployed becomes a critical factor in determining the lifespan of a new application. The Transcend phase is about helping an organization to deploy a continual process improvement loop for the application itself. With premise-based software, where the cost of change is high and where upgrades are few and far between, this can be difficult. No doubt about it, in the SaaS world, which lends itself much more to the concept of a living system, this can become a continuous process.

This is where we drive adoption. (Our methodology does not allow for even the possibility of shelfware.) Included in this step is the delivery of user training, on-demand learning, change management, the creation of centers of excellence with the client, and the establishment of an application governance process. To ensure data quality, we conduct a phased rollout, establish data input conventions, and set up a duplicate record strategy and a data enrichment strategy. At this point, the project is delivering real business value as defined in the success plan, and the client is realizing a return on investment.

Does it sound too simple to believe? Compared to the conventional consulting process it certainly does. But we have done this hundreds of times for companies as diverse as The DuPont Corporation, The Hartford

Insurance Company, and The General Electric Company, and it works. In very short sprints, this process lets us deliver a fully working production application that provides immediate business value and meets the client's success criteria. The following graphics show how we handle various issues as we follow the Translate, Transform, Transcend process.

Data Quality Planning—Data Migration Process

Stage	Tasks	Bluewolf Phase
Data Planning	Data from source systems	Translate
	Success criteria for rollout	
	Ongoing considerations	
Data Execution	Resource Utilization	Transform
	Enabling Technologies * ESI / DRE	
	Ensuring successful go-live	
Data Quality On-going	Phased rollouts	Transcend
	Data input conventions	
	Duplicate record strategy	
	Data enrichment strategy	

Source: Bluewolf Group

Education, Adoption, Change Management Process

Stage	Tasks	Phase
Planning	Change management	Translate
	Success criteria and measurement	
	Communication Strategy	
Development	Custom Curriculum	Transform
	Adoption Materials	
	Global Logistics	
	UAT	
Execution	Training Delivery	Transcend
	Continuing Education	
	On Demand Learning	
	In the Path of Work	

Source: Bluewolf Group

Translate, Transform, Transcend is Bluewolf's inherent process, but we are not suggesting that it is the only way to deliver true value in a software consulting project. Rather, we use it as an example of what needs to take place in a successful project, and it is simple in its 3-step approach. This is key. Traditional development methodologies are stacked with phases upon phases, and task sets, each numbered and ordered. That approach is doomed from the start because it presupposes that there is a cookbook with a one-size-fits-all recipe for delivering a successful project. Bluewolf's 3-step approach only presupposes one thing: *There are **three** distinct exercises that define successful change—whether it is in software, hiring, process improvement, or for that matter, anything in corporate America.*

If you ask groups of people to rally around 8-step improvement processes or 30-step change management exercises, you'll lose at least half of your audience before you even get started. Groups do things well in threes. People can generally remember the three main points of a presentation or a project. And in any given project, three things are key at the macro level:

1. **Translate:** In other words, let's talk about what the heck you are trying to accomplish.
2. **Transform:** Let's take the leap of faith and go and get it done, keeping an eye on what we learned in the Translate stage, while allowing for emerging requirements.
3. **Transcend:** Let's make sure what we devise sticks and gets better, and is measurable and repeatable.

So where does our magic fail?

We don't recommend trying to build a bridge with it, or a nuclear reactor. In other words, there are certain projects that are not well served by a model that welcomes emerging and changing requirements, and where certain risks and contingencies need to be scripted to cover the risk of even one bad decision. But for 99% of business software projects, it's ideal.

How does our agile approach work for HR and recruiting? Again:

1. **Translate:** What skills do you need, for how long, working on what project, and for what price?

2. **Transform:** Let's find 10 qualified candidates, and screen, reference-check, prepare, interview, and select them.

3. **Transcend:** Let's get them on-site, get them acquainted with the project, and get them productive. We'll also figure out what additional value they can bring to the organization.

Then we'll engage in the recruiting process again, to ensure that we're always equipped to deliver the right resource at the right time, quickly and on a continual basis; some think of this as right-sizing and right-sourcing.

If you don't believe there are new ways to approach old problems, check out the comparison of internal vs. remote DBAs published by the Meta Group, which was acquired by Gartner. At that time, 2003, Meta Group found the total cost of maintenance of the remote solution was just $84,000 compared to $226,000 for an internal solution. Thinking about what you actually need to achieve, and trying a different way to achieve it can get you what you need *and* save you money.

Now that you have glimpsed our methodology, let's look more closely at the agile consulting process.

14

The Agile Consulting Process

We have spent considerable time disparaging the waterfall methodology. In truth, it was a valid attempt to apply some order to early software development efforts for which there was no process at all. The idea of business computing—that almost every business could have access to software that would facilitate its business processes—was new, and nobody understood the best way to do it. Back then people were trying to figure it out as they went. Craig Larman, in fact, suggests that the initial waterfall methodology was more iterative than its later, common usage suggests, and that it was meant for the most simple and straightforward projects, not complex software development. Regardless of its origins, the waterfall process became widely accepted as a single-pass process, even by those who weren't comfortable with it. It became, in short, the de facto standard methodology for software development.

You can appreciate what was going on at that time. Computing resources—including CPUs, network bandwidth, and storage—were extremely costly. The waterfall methodology, with its process akin to measuring the lumber five times before making one cut, made sense.

These resources were too costly to waste on mistakes. Today, however, the costs of CPU cycles, network bandwidth, and storage are rapidly dropping to unprecedented lows. Most companies can easily afford to burn these resources on multiple iterations in order to get to something that does what they want. Besides, even if they're satisfied with the project outcome, they may still want or need something changed or adjusted six months down the road. Painstakingly measuring five times to cut once makes no sense. In an agile, iterative situation, it makes more sense to measure and cut, measure and cut, and measure and cut repeatedly.

The problem with the waterfall methodology as it came to be practiced was that the massive, detailed requirements documents at the heart of the process—the equivalent of measuring five (or 50) times before making one cut—didn't work. In the time it took to take those measurements, the project continued to change. Maybe the repeated measurements were intended to ensure a consistent result, but they never did. People kept adding or changing requirements. Every time someone went back to take new measurements, they got a different result. Eventually the consultants or client ran out of time, money, or patience, and just built the system based on what they had, the last measurement or the first measurement or whatever, it didn't really matter. They were all wrong (or right, depending on who took the measurement and when). The waterfall approach was doomed to fail, irrelevant before the first line of code was written.

More importantly from our agile consulting standpoint, while the waterfall approach captured huge amounts of desired functionality, it failed to capture what the business actually needed to achieve with the effort. There was no success planning, no definition of what management expected to gain from this investment. For example, the waterfall requirements document for a CRM application might list hundreds of pages of individual functions. Yet, there would be no clear, simple statement like: "We expect to end up with a consolidated sales pipeline, and a single clear view of everything in the pipeline along with its current status." Without that clear definition of success, you could build in every single function and still not have a successful project.

Our agile consulting methodology looks only a few steps ahead. We define the success plan at the outset and then sketch out the next few steps. We prioritize each step toward the success goal on the basis of impact and cost—we figure out what will give us the most impact on our goal at a reasonable cost and within a reasonable timeframe, such as 30 days. This leads us to our Eleventh Law of Consulting Economics: *Every project must start with a specific success plan.* Without it, you have no idea what you are driving toward.

It sounds simple, but the fact of the matter is that most companies get caught up in the feature-function discussion before they define success criteria. This is a huge mistake. The 21st century consultant can better serve by discussing success criteria, rather than trying to define every intricate feature in a project.

As they say, when you don't know where you are going, any road will take you there. Well, we insist on knowing where our clients want us to go. There may be multiple ways to get there, and the iterative approach will lead us to the best one, but it's definitely not true that just any road will do.

Craig Larman describes agile development as methods that "apply timeboxed iterative and evolutionary development, adaptive planning, promote[s] evolutionary delivery, and include other values and practices that encourage *agility,*" which he goes on to define as rapid and flexible response to change.

Characteristics of agile consulting mirror those of agile development, and include:

> **Focus on the success plan;**
> **Light rather than heavy control (no Command and Control);**
> **Continuous collaboration;**
> **Teamwork, team decision-making, self-direction;**
> **Transparency;**
> **Simple rules;**
> **Direct, active client involvement;**
> **Regular feedback and communication;**
> **Empirical, dynamic processes.**

Finally, although our focus as consultants is on IT and business software, agile consulting often has a distinctly low tech, high touch cast. We prefer phone calls to email and face-to-face dialog rather than phone calls. It's not that we don't use email or IM, shared online space, or other high tech, collaborative tools. To the contrary, we may use them quite heavily, but our default is to always go with the most high touch way that's practical.

So how does this agile consulting methodology work in practice? Walk with us through a typical engagement.

We start the engagement with a face-to-face meeting involving the client and our team, which at this point consists of no more than two or possibly three of our people, along with one or two of the client's people. Together we start talking about the success plan. We find out what the client wants to achieve, specifically, from this effort. Many answer that they want more sales or greater profits. Of course, we're talking about a software project, and we're business software consultants. Software, in most cases, doesn't *make* sales, and increased sales don't always translate into greater profits. So many variables that are far beyond the scope of the software are brought to the table. So we explain that the success plan has to define success *in terms of what the software can impact,* such as ease of pulling together disparate data, improved visibility into the sales pipeline, increased ability to ensure that opportunities are not falling through the cracks in the process, or reducing the number of process handoffs.

Out of this meeting and subsequent discussions, we develop the success plan, along with the agreed-upon metrics that will tell everybody involved—both client and consultant—when we have succeeded. A success metric is simple, such as a reduction in the number of mishandled inquiries. We also discuss the functional requirements.

Let's say this client has a success goal of moving to a single sales management system. Until now, the client has used a combination of multiple systems and different spreadsheets. Needless to say, the client contends with conflicting data, an inability to get consolidated reports quickly, and all the other complications that multiple systems produce. The success plan calls for moving everyone over to a single platform.

By the next meeting we are ready to discuss possible designs. We'll have plotted out the next few steps that will move us to our agreed-upon success goal. In this iteration, we think we can pin down a couple of key functions that are high on the client's priority list. Since we have done work like this hundreds of times, we may even be able to bring in a working application—or several—that are similar to what the client may ultimately end up with. We settle on the initial design and define the timebox for the delivery of the initial functions, say three weeks.

Three weeks later we return with a working iteration. It doesn't do everything the client wants, but the client can actually use it to do meaningful work. Now everybody knows we're on the right track. At the meeting we discuss some possible changes in the layout and configuration of the current application, as well as the next few functions we want to add. Again, we set the timebox, another three weeks. We're off and running.

We return with the next iteration, but this time, the meeting goes differently. The client wants to change the scope of the project. That's OK. Our methodology is agile, remember? It can accommodate change. As we work through the changes with the client, it becomes apparent to everybody that the client's original process may have to change too. Now we define the next iteration, but focus more on this one issue. We give ourselves a two-week timebox and we agree to a daily 10-minute call among all the parties to stay on top of what appears to be a situation in flux.

Two weeks later, after a bit of a sprint in the last week of the timebox, we return with an iteration that works. Now we're back on track again. We also decide to bring in one of our data specialists to hammer out a data integration problem. At the same time we begin to develop the training curriculum and materials.

The following graphic shows the entire Translate, Transform, Transcend agile consulting process.

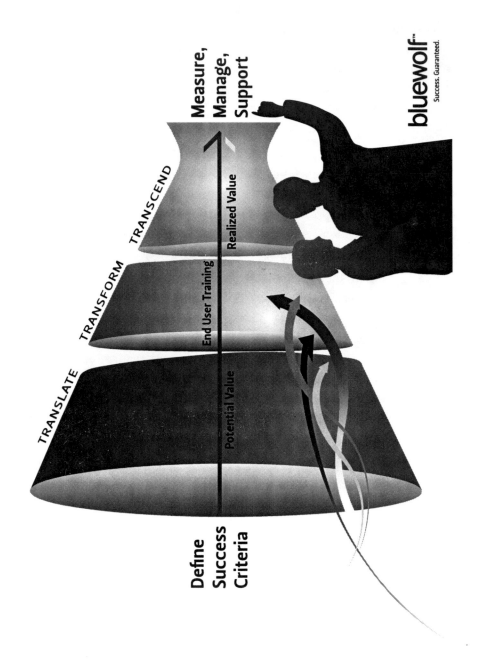

In this case the client was able to go live in five months. Sometimes we can complete a project in three or four months. Rarely do we go past six months. Also notice the Success Plan Realization in month six. This is part of our guarantee. At this stage, we review the metrics we defined in the success plan. Our guarantee is based on meeting those metrics. If we don't, we keep working at the success goals on our dime until those metrics are met. We have to say we have never failed to meet the success metrics. It's not because we are brilliant or lucky. Rather, it is thanks to our agile consulting process. If the project is not achieving the agreed upon success metrics, we become aware of it early. We sit down with the client and analyze the situation. Maybe the metrics were wrong to begin with, or maybe the requested functionality was wrong. Whatever the problem, we talk through the solution and make adjustments sooner rather than later to ensure the success plan is achieved. And, of course, if we have to stay on the job another iteration longer to meet those metrics, then we do it at our expense. That's our guarantee. See what kind of guarantee the big consulting firms offer.

Elements of the Agile Development Process

> **Success planning**

> **Continuous client hands-on involvement**

> **Ongoing communications, frequent dialogue**

> **Fast iterations**

> **Training planning and development from the start**

> **Success guarantees**

So far, we have been talking about consulting and technology industry trends, methodologies, and processes. Although we've made a few references to client work, we haven't yet shown you much of it. In the next chapter we will start to illustrate how the agile consulting process works when applied to real clients with real business problems.

15
Client Experience

In this chapter, we look at how the agile consulting client experience differs from the client experience with big, conventional firms. We also discuss the client's responsibilities in contributing to the success of the project engagement. Up until now, we've criticized the big consulting firms for their roles in the software failures of the past. In fairness, they weren't the only ones at fault. Clients were complicit with the firms' processes, even though, had they stayed on top of things as they should have, they'd have had numerous opportunities to pull the plug on projects gone awry. So our process includes something we've never seen before, despite all the management conferences we've attended: A checklist of client responsibilities, that spells out the things the client needs to do to help ensure a successful engagement. (This is not a Customer Bill of Rights, something that's becoming quite popular in many industries. A consulting customer's Bill of Rights is simple: It ensures software that works as promised, and delivers business value on time—within 30, 60, or 90 days max—at a fair price.) Rather, what we are talking about here (and including below), is a checklist of things the client must bring to the project.

The big, conventional consulting firms viewed the client's account as a never-ending meal ticket. They maintained a ruse of concern that the vendors didn't care about the client (although they didn't beat up on the vendors too hard, since they enjoyed long-established, preferred partner relationships with many of them). However, the firms were as bad as, or worse than, the vendors in regard to the client experience. They liked to pay lip service to the idea of the consultant as an independent advisor, who would give the client honest advice without a vested interest in any particular vendor. Maybe that was true on some level, but only to the extent that the consulting firm didn't actually work directly for, or maintain a partner relationship with, any particular vendor.

The consultant's advice and guidance was totally skewed, if not toward a particular vendor, then certainly toward the consulting firm's own interests. Sure, the consultants promised independent, unbiased advice. But if the consulting firm had, say, 300 trained Oracle consultants sitting on the bench waiting for a new project, you can bet the firm's recommendations, presented honestly and sincerely, would point invariably toward an Oracle solution. Oracle provides a good, if somewhat pricey product, yet it serves well in most cases. So maybe the Oracle recommendation was honestly arrived at. Still, we always wonder if the same consulting firm had a few hundred spare SAP experts sitting around twiddling their thumbs, would they have just as sincerely presented an SAP solution? We know that we could easily argue the case.

Agile consulting firms, on the other hand, focus on the client's business success and on delivering specific, measurable business value. Only by focusing on the client's business and delivering business value do we get our meal ticket punched. Every recommendation is driven by what is best for the client and the success of the project. In our particular case, since we offer an unusual guarantee, we cannot afford to do it any other way. What is best for the client is indeed best for the agile consulting firm, even if we might have honest disagreements about the ideal way to proceed. Those disagreements arise from different ideas of how best to achieve business results, not from any vested interest on the part of the consultant. Just check out the box about our experience with GoodTimes.

In the meantime, here's a different real life story, only this time the names and geography have been changed to protect the guilty. A large West Coast manufacturing company, recently acquired by a larger manufacturer in Sweden, needed to modernize its approach to CRM. It didn't have a specific CRM system. Instead it used a wide range of different tools to cobble together something that provided some CRM functions. Its managers didn't know the CRM market, the products seemed costly, and the risks involved in the decision were, admittedly, considerable. As prudent managers, they decided to bring in a giant consulting firm to analyze their needs and recommend the best CRM solution. (Management, it seems, can never be faulted for making a wrong decision, if the decision in question was to bring in a top-tier consulting firm that made a stupid recommendation.) As it turned out, this world-class consulting firm had recently acquired another consulting firm with hundreds of Siebel consultants, who now wondered what would happen to them in the wake of the acquisition.

The parent manufacturing company back in Sweden already had standardized on Salesforce.com (SFC) and was very satisfied with it. For some reason, the U.S. managers were not aware of this. Anyway, after collecting $800,000 in consulting fees, the consulting firm returned months later with a recommendation to—surprise, surprise—implement the Siebel CRM. Did the consulting firm know of the rumors that Siebel would be acquired shortly and absorbed into Oracle? There hadn't been an official announcement, although for months, the *Wall Street Journal* had repeatedly mentioned the possibility. We guess that must not be a publication the firm's partners or consultants ever read.

Maybe the Siebel solution was an honest recommendation arrived at after months of interviewing and analysis. However, forgive us if we're skeptical. The only thing that impresses us about this story was the exquisite timing of the consulting firm. They managed to wring out months of consulting, and made their recommendation just a few weeks before Oracle publicly confirmed the acquisition of Siebel, which effectively rendered the Siebel recommendation instantly moot. Still, it was a valiant effort to milk the final few hundred thousand dollars from their Siebel practice, and possibly capture one last multi-year Siebel engagement for hundreds of their Siebel consultants who would otherwise look to acquire new skills—or start waiting tables. If they could have, you can bet, they would have milked the engagement even longer—at least until they could have morphed it into a multi-year Oracle migration project costing millions more.

In the wake of this fiasco, the U.S. managers suddenly realized that SFC was already in place at the parent company, and it was doing everything they wanted for a tiny fraction of the cost of the recommended Siebel system. (Full disclosure: we helped with the U.S. rollout of SFC.)

It was events like this that made us think carefully about what constitutes a client's management responsibility. But before we get into that, let's just finish this last thought about recommendations: There are no unbiased observers, especially among conventional consulting firms that maintain large rosters of highly paid people with particular skills. The consulting firms that maintain stables of consultants either need to keep them employed, or let them go (and the latter is an unpleasant and costly undertaking). Managers who think otherwise might just as well believe in the tooth fairy.

The truth is, we wouldn't be any different, except for one huge distinction—we don't keep armies of consultants on our roster. This fact forces us to actually turn down engagements that don't correspond with the skills we have. If you came to us, for instance, asking for help in implementing a geographic information system or an integrated emergency 911 system, we'd wish you luck and decline the project, because that's not what we do.

This leads us to our Twelfth Law of Consulting Economics: *Play to your strengths.* The costs of maintaining deep skills across too many disciplines are shockingly high in many ways. Personnel costs, of course, are high. It takes too much effort to find and retain those resources. And, most importantly, the costs of the compromises you will have to make in dealing with your clients are way too high. It is better for your client, your bottom line, your integrity, and your mental health, to know your strengths and play to them.

Now, about client responsibilities and the client-consultant relationship that is at the heart of the client experience: We like to say that agile consulting firms have to focus on the client, but we're really talking about more than some vague, silly, feel-good, I'm-okay-you're-okay kind of thing. Agile firms have to focus on delivering specific business value to the client. That is built into the agile consulting methodology from day one. The success plan does nothing but focus everybody on client business value. The daily and weekly stand-up meetings revolve purely around achieving the success criteria for the current iteration. Fast iterations and timeboxing all are intended to focus the team on delivering business value to the client. Finally, our guarantee is simply a mechanism to ensure we keep client focus by delivering the business value that we agreed upon from the outset, in collaboration with the client.

In addition to staying client-focused and knowing our strengths, as agile consultants, we are willing to disagree with the client. Ultimately, that both benefits the client, and enhances their experience with us. Remember, with agile consulting the client is actively engaged on a weekly basis as the team thrashes out each iteration and plans for the next one. There are always different ways to proceed, and is not unusual that our people and the client disagree. But there is a difference between partnering with clients and sucking up to them. A good salesman may be taught that the client is always right; a good consultant, however, should never follow that dictum. Certainly the client knows its business, its products, its customers, and its market. That does not mean the client automatically knows the best way to proceed on an IT project. The consultant is brought in to give honest guidance based on skills and relevant experiences that the client does not have. The best way to proceed comes out of the give and take between the client and the consulting team.

This leads us to our Thirteenth Law of Consulting Economics: *Be ready and willing to fight hard (and fairly) for what you feel is best.* However, there is a corollary to this law: If you lose the fight (and sometimes you will), lose graciously and continue to do your very best for the client.

> *GoodTimes, a self-help and entertainment video distribution company, embarked on a multi-year, multi-phase effort to modernize its IT systems by deploying Oracle's suite of applications. We weren't initially involved. However, when the Oracle efforts started to sputter we were brought in.*
>
> *At about the same time their Oracle troubles began, GoodTimes got hit with a second whammy. Wal-Mart, a huge customer, was changing its Electronic Data Interchange (EDI) standard,*

and GoodTimes had to comply fast. So we took on the EDI proj-ect too. Not long afterward, the company realized it also had to modernize its Web platforms. (Did you notice? No SFC in sight.)

By now we were deeply engaged with multiple projects for GoodTimes. As you can imagine, this was an important customer we didn't want to lose. However, everything almost came to a crashing end with the Web platform upgrade. We strongly rec-ommended a custom application built on top of Microsoft's .Net. GoodTimes, however, was already committed to ATG's ecom-merce system, and the two didn't go together at all. It had to be one or the other. We argued hard for the .Net approach know-ing that we risked losing the client's business. Things got a little testy at one point.

Sure, we had .Net skills. We also had resources that knew ATG, just as we had resources that knew Oracle. We weren't arguing based on a vested interest in .Net. Our only vested interest was giving the client the best advice and delivering a successful Web platform, which we hoped would lead to even more projects (al-though it was looking doubtful at this point, because things had gotten so heated).

Anyway, the client pulled rank and ordered the ATG approach. We went along in the end and made it happen. The Web platform worked (.Net would have worked better in our opinion, although we never brought it up again).

The frequent, highly engaged (but less heated) dialogue pro-cess that came out of that argument, however, became a regu-lar part of every GoodTimes project. And yes, there were more projects—a CRM initiative, a business intelligence project, and a data warehouse management and data integration project. That adds up to a lot of business, and we believe we won it because 1) we delivered business value fast and at a fair price, and 2) the client respected us because we were willing to disagree—and recognized we would always tell them the truth.

Unlike conventional consulting, the agile consulting process imposes a number of responsibilities on the client. Some of these are almost too embarrassing to mention, and are the management equivalent of remind-ing people to brush their teeth. For example, the client has the responsibility for making sound business decisions. We didn't think we had to remind clients about that, but some clients make really stupid choices. For example, how could the managers at the West Coast manufacturing company bring in the big global consulting firm—and spend $800K— before exploring what their parent company used for CRM and how it was working? That had to be either laziness or incompetence.

Related to that is the need for the client's managers to get involved in project decision-making. That doesn't mean micro-managing the project. It means they have to want to know what is going on. Agile consulting requires the active participation of the client's people. Some clients don't like agile consulting, at least at first, for that very reason; because it requires their active, direct involvement. They resent the time and resources it takes to be involved. They also don't like the responsibility because it means they have to share the blame if something goes wrong. (They don't understand the Agile consulting team concept and how credit or blame is a shared responsibility.) They would prefer that we just went off—like a big consulting company—and make every decision for them, build the project, and come back with a ready-to-run application, no sweat, no fuss on their part.

Of course, the big consulting companies promise to do just that, except the results never work as promised and the cost is astronomical. Agile consulting works; it delivers business value fast and at an affordable price. However, it requires the active involvement of the client. And part of the reason it works so well is that the client assumes some of the responsibility. Along the way, the client also learns a huge amount about the internal workings of the project, how to maintain it, and how to enhance it. This knowledge transfer, embedded within the agile consulting process, plays a key role in our ability to deliver software that works at an affordable price. (You'll learn more about that in the next chapter, where we'll discuss agile consulting's financial model.)

Client involvement is essential when it comes to prioritizing. In every project, there is more value available than the consultant will have the time or resources to deliver. Every piece of software has more functionality than the client needs or should use, at least at the outset. As a result, priorities must be set. And only the client—specifically the client's executive project champion—can effectively set those priorities. Precisely because the choices are business priorities, absolutely NO ONE other than the client's executive project champion and his or her fellow executives should be setting the priorities.

Similarly, the client also has to make an effort to interview every resource the consultant puts on the project. Thankfully, an agile consulting team is very small—just a handful of people. But because the team is small and will be working very closely with the client's people, chemistry is vitally important. The agile consulting process depends on teamwork, trust, and honest communication. We have several hundred resources on our roster as we write this. There are individuals on our roster who are loved by some clients more than anything, while others hate the same resource. Go figure. In the end, much of it boils down to personal chemistry. We don't care who we ultimately assign to a project as long as the team works. Therefore, the client has the responsibility to get involved in the chemistry mix to make sure the team works smoothly. And the time to do this is at the very start of the project. Like prioritizing, this is another thing we cannot do for the client.

Another part of client involvement is the requirement for ongoing communication between the client and the consulting team. We've mentioned this in previous chapters. In large part, communication sets the agile consulting process apart from conventional consulting. Preferably, this communication happens in person or by phone. Email, IM, and online collaboration have their uses, but nothing replaces real-time, live communication to convey urgency and emotion, and to avoid misunderstandings. As we said in our Eighth Law of Consulting Economics: *When it comes to success, communication is everything.*

Yet another thing the client needs to bring to the table is the willingness to exercise executive authority. Every software project involves change, and change always generates some resistance. At some point, the executive champion must be willing and able to use his or her authority to force adoption of the change. We feel we win over adoption through communication and by showing results. In the end, most people want to buy in. Still, there always are the rare resisters who must be ordered to comply, and the executive champion must be willing and able to give that order.

In the previous chapter, we talked about our guarantee. It is simply not possible to offer a guarantee like ours without the involvement of the project champion and the rest of the client's team. Without client involvement in success plans, without priorities, without checking for team chemistry, you cannot deliver a project on time or at budget that meets the client's success metrics. In fact, you won't even know what the success metrics are. If you don't know where you're going, any road could get you there. That's why the conventional consulting firms don't guarantee anything and couldn't meet a guarantee if they tried; they haven't a clue where the client needs to go. (And they don't really care since the engagement is only tangentially about the client's needs anyway; it is about the big consulting firm's needs.) Because the agile consulting process so integrally involves the client, we can offer a guarantee that makes sense to everybody involved—and meet it.

Here is what the client must bring to the consulting engagement if it is to be successful:

> **Good business judgment;**

> **An executive as the active project champion;**

> **Involvement in interviewing team members;**

> **Involvement in determining success criteria;**

> **Ability to set priorities;**

> **Regular participation in team dialogue;**

> **Ability and willingness to exercise executive authority.**

We have spent a lot of time in this book beating up the big consulting firms for their bloated business models. In the next chapter we will take a look at the agile consulting financial model. This is why we can deliver more business value faster and at less cost than the conventional firms, and still make a handsome profit for ourselves.

16

The Agile Consulting Financial Model

In this chapter we are going to discuss how an agile consulting firm like ours manages to deliver projects that provide value, and how we do it on time, at a substantially lower cost than that of the big consulting firms. Once you see how we do it, you will realize that there is no magic here. Like the Wizard of Oz, we might be sorry that we've pulled back the curtain. We guess we'll just have to deal with that later.

So how do we deliver value for less than the big consulting firms? Fair question. Let's start by declaring three facts from the start:

1. **Our people are paid as much as, or more than, their counterparts at big consulting firms.**
2. **Our partners take profits just like partners at the conventional firms.**
3. **Our business is quite profitable, and we intend for it to stay that way.**

As you can see, we are not offering our services as a loss leader. We pay our people and ourselves well, and we expect to make money on every project and engagement. We are not running a charity (although we give extensively to charity). In fact, beware of consulting firms that bid an engagement at an obviously low rate. You will get what you pay for, one way or another. Either they intend to make back their low-ball quote—and more—on subsequent changes and support, or they lack the necessary skills or industry experience, and intend use you as the guinea pig while they acquire those skills and/or seek to gain industry credibility. If your consultants are not making money on your project, then something is wrong, and you are probably at risk.

Of course, one way to make money while offering a low price is to ship the work off to a low-cost development center overseas. In this case, the developers actually *do* get paid less, but there are other costs and complications to consider. As we discussed previously, those low-cost offshore deals may not turn out to be as cheap as expected, once you factor in all of the hidden costs and project complexity. We don't ship work offshore, although we do utilize some functions as a remote managed service. The savings there are legitimate; we can spread the cost of a specialist, such as a DBA, over multiple clients, none of whom need the specialized service full-time.

This brings us back to the original question: If we are not cutting our rates and we are not offshoring chunks of our clients' jobs, how do we deliver software that produces business value for less than the conventional firms?

We'll start with an anecdote. One of our first clients was Primedia Inc., a multi-billion dollar, multi-division company that ordinarily wouldn't look at a consulting firm like us—at least not the way we looked back then. In fact, they didn't; they had already contracted with KPMG (now BearingPoint) to implement an Oracle ERP system. They wouldn't have even spoken to us, except we happened to call the day they received a $5 million estimate from KPMG for the ERP implementation.

We estimated that we could do the first phase of the job in three months, for $250,000. We tackled the corporate group first, which ensured the foundation was in place for the other Primedia divisions that would roll out later. Our approach to this project was simple: We'd take the KPMG project, which was all-encompassing and touched every division and process in the Primedia empire, and do it the agile way. Instead of building in and billing for a ton of full-time resources and overhead to cover any potential risk, we split things up into a series of smaller, achievable, projects. We moved from the corporate group, to the B2B group, then to the consumer group, and the About.com division, and built everything on the same foundation.

All told, within 18 months, Primedia's ERP system was rolled out to the entire company, at a price tag that was roughly half of the $5 million estimate that KPMG had tossed out. Better than that, our client stood in front of his Board just three months after we started and bragged about how the ERP system had already gone live for the corporate entity.

So, how do we do it cheaper? The answer, as before, comes back to the agile consulting process. We use small teams, short iterations, and leverage client involvement. Where a big consulting firm might send at least a dozen people to gather requirements and study your business processes, we send two or three people, who work with your people. After all, they are the ones who are supposed to know your business processes. You shouldn't have to pay us to re-discover the wheel. You save thousands or even tens of thousands of dollars, and weeks or months on a project, just by eliminating the need for us to figure out what you already know.

The agile process also requires us to define specific functional deliverables that provide measurable business value with all iterations. That means just a few weeks into the process, clients start capturing some of the ROI they expect the new system to deliver, while we use that success to jump-start the next iteration. Conventional firms using the waterfall methodology don't begin to deliver any value for months or even years, if ever. With the agile method, the costs are lower and the returns come faster. You can do the math yourself. Furthermore, our use of success plans, combined with the prioritizing that we do with the project champion, ensures that the functionality we deliver from day one—with the first iteration and every iteration thereafter—is functionality that the client made a priority.

Agile's iterative, timeboxed approach also keeps costs down. When we are on the spot to deliver functionality in 30 or 60 days there is no time to waste. We stay focused and work in the most efficient way. If a chunk of functionality can't be delivered within a given timebox, we drop the lowest priority part of that functionality, so when the timebox expires, we can still deliver usable functionality. Maybe you won't get all you expected, but what you do get, you can put right to work. And what was dropped will follow in the next iteration, which might be just two weeks later.

The expression "time is money" certainly has never been truer than with agile consulting. Everyone is driven to deliver quantifiable value fast. You probably have also heard another expression: "You can have it fast, cheap, or good—pick any two." This expression refers to the tradeoffs that must be made between speed, cost, and quality. Agile consulting lets you have it all—you can actually have speed and quality cheap! This isn't some kind of black magic or sleight-of-hand trickery. What you sacrifice is scope. If you planned on getting certain functionality in the next 60-day iteration for, say, $50,000, and we had to drop one piece of functionality to finish within the timebox, then yes, you received a little less scope, and less functionality, for your money. But what you did receive was fast, of good quality, and within your approved budget. Or put another way: you got fast, good, AND cheap. No having to pick two.

So how did this work in the Primedia case? To start, our iterative approach encouraged Primedia to take more tasks upon themselves over time. We were giving up some revenue, but we figured we would make more in the long run from a satisfied client.

Second, we used expert resources that did not have to be trained, and who had the very specific skill sets necessary to set up the application, build integrations, convert data, and train users. This allowed us to work faster and deliver quicker, while negating the risk that exists when a project team is staffed with unqualified individuals. The resources we used had an average of 10 years of experience. And, because our model does not require us to pay partners millions of dollars for managing spreadsheets, our rates were 50% to 70% of those quoted by KPMG. At the same time our people were paid as well as, if not better than, KPMG's (and our partners still collected their profits at the end of the year).

Lastly, we used the agile approach. We met with the team (originally three Bluewolf resources and two client resources, more later on as the team expanded) daily, and we recited our deliverables to each other on a continual basis. We set up a knowledge base that everyone had access to throughout the project. And we delivered working software quickly. First we demonstrated a conference pilot within the first two weeks, and later provided several iterations that users could test and tweak as they wished.

As with any project, our variables were threefold: Time (the most precious), dollars, and scope. Only one of them—the scope—could fluctuate. As promised, we met the 90-day deadline, and the project went live and into its Transcend phase. The client was amazed. We had just done something unthinkable in the big consulting world. That's the agile consulting process.

Another way our agile consulting process saves clients money is through the use of SaaS products. When people think of SaaS, they think of Salesforce.com. We are one of the leading Salesforce.com implementation firms, but we realize it is not the only SaaS product out there. At the time of this writing, ThinkStrategies announced that its SaaS Showplace online directory (http://www.saas-showplace.com/) included over 1300 applications spread across 80 application, industry, and enabling technology categories, and that it was adding new applications every month. If Salesforce.com doesn't work for a client, there are plenty of other SaaS applications to choose from.

SaaS meshes unusually well with the agile consulting approach. It saves huge amounts of money because the basic coding and testing is already in place. You can demonstrate functional code within days. And because there's no need to burn time and money reinventing code, iterations can follow each other quickly. Very little custom coding is ever actually required, because most customization can be handled through configuration. Remember the West Coast manufacturer we discussed in the last chapter? By the time it would have licensed, customized, and deployed the Siebel application the consulting firm had recommended, it would have wasted at least two years and millions of dollars. Instead, for a tiny fraction of the cost of a Siebel implementation, it ended up with Salesforce.com, which was up and running and delivering value in mere weeks. We wouldn't be surprised if that $800,000 consulting fee for a misguided, ultimately worthless Siebel recommendation was, by far, the biggest expense in their adoption of CRM.

Finally, the agile consulting process saves the client money by transferring knowledge of how to deploy, maintain, and enhance the application long into the future. First, the SaaS provider makes all of the big enhancements automatically. If tax codes or reporting mandates change, or if customers request particular functionality, the SaaS vendor routinely builds those things into the next upgrade, which might be 30 or 60 days away. Customers log in one day and the change is there; they didn't have to do a thing, not even take out their checkbooks.

If you do have to change something, however, because maybe your business suddenly changed, you can do that yourself, too. Since you have worked with your consultants closely throughout the initial configuration, deployment, and rollout, and actively engaged in a constant dialog, you are more than ready to take over. Something about your business changes, no problem. Just reconfigure that part of the application. Your in-house team can probably do it as two-week iteration while you keep your checkbook inside the desk.

As an agile consulting firm, this is where we miss out on the big bucks the conventional consulting firms get. Those drawn-out maintenance and enhancement engagements could keep conventional consulting teams going long enough to put their children through college, maybe even grad school. Maybe someday if we don't have enough new consulting engagements to keep us busy, we will regret adopting the agile process. Although somehow, we don't think that day will ever come in our lifetimes, or those of our children.

Now you know how we make money at this. There is no magic here. SaaS certainly plays a big part in cutting costs. Even without SaaS, however, we focus strictly on what delivers business value, and we cut out everything that would only slow the project down and add to its cost. We avoid reinventing the wheel wherever possible. By insisting on client involvement and transferring skills to the client, in effect we shift costs onto the client. These costs, however, are exactly the kinds of costs the client wants to control. At the point when the knowledge transfer has been completed, the client will be able to do the job with total ownership and control, better and for less than any consulting company could.

Comparison: Conventional vs. Agile Consulting Costs

The following table will make clear just where Agile consulting combined with SaaS can really reduce costs. The only place where the conventional approach has any advantage is in the area of application integration, but that's only because a bunch of infrastructure integration costs have to be picked up for the first time. Still, in the end, we're talking about huge savings with Agile over conventional consulting.

Cost factors	Conventional	Agile
Planning and Design	$20,000	$16,520
Infrastructure and Maintenance	$142,814	$0
Deployment	$217,400	$146,900
Application Integration	$19,500	$62,715
Training	$20,000	$20,000
Total Solution Cost (consulting and software)	$419,774	$246,135

Source: Bluewolf Group

Note: The Agile costs assume the implementation of a SaaS solution. The conventional costs assume the deployment of a traditional enterprise CRM solution.

We promised this book was going to be about business process and not about technology, and that's where we've pretty much kept the focus. However, in the next chapter we are going to talk about technology and how it supports the agile process. Bear with us. There will be no bits and bytes babble. We'll be taking a high-level view.

17
On the Technology Edge

We know, we know; we promised this book wasn't going to be about technology yet here we are with a chapter on it. Today, however, almost anything you talk about will come around to technology sooner or later. True to form, at this point, a little discussion about technology is now in order, and we hope it won't hurt too much. We also are including collaboration—the central topic in the next chapter—as part of this overall discussion, because technology certainly facilitates collaboration, and collaboration is central to agile consulting.

We frequently hear executives complain about technology as they wistfully dream of some idealized, pre-technology business world. This usually happens when their zillion-dollar software project has just imploded, or when they've received a shock-inducing invoice from their consulting firm for a project that still isn't finished, has no end in sight, and is already far over budget. Or, it happens when auditors are beating them up over security, or disaster recovery, or compliance.

Let's face it: Technology can be a royal pain in the "rump." It can be costly and demanding of frequent attention. It can be bewildering and frustrating and distracting and disruptive. IT people, vendors, and consultants can seem like a completely different species, speaking an entirely different language from your own. Plenty of people out there even wonder why they put up with it. If they could get rid of it, they would in a flash.

The truth is you cannot get rid of IT. There is no going back to some mythical pre-IT business Garden of Eden. Businesses cannot compete in the 21st century without a lot of IT support. (That's really been true since the last quarter of the 20th century.) There is no way you can drive your business processes fast enough, with sufficient quality, and at a price customers will pay, without IT. You can't do even the simplest thing, like return a customer's phone call, without IT. The first time somebody asks a question that requires you to access information—almost any information—your dream of running the business without IT will instantly end. Increasingly, your revenue stream—the lifeblood of your business—will be directly tied to IT. Every revenue-generating activity—sales, production, delivery, customer service—relies on IT.

To survive in the 21st century global marketplace, we all must live on the technology edge, whether we like it or not. It is the only way modern business is conducted. Agile consultants understand the value of technology even as they concentrate their focus on the client's business process. A key part of their responsibility, in fact, is to make sure that the technology serves and supports the client's unique business processes to the greatest extent possible—and to pick the simplest path to get there.

Our Second Law of Consulting Economics says that a successful business process trumps cool technology, and we dearly embrace that. It doesn't mean, however, that cool technology can't help a business process, even invigorate it. We look to technology wherever we can find it, from dragging business rules out of obsolete legacy systems, to applying the most leading-edge applications to support and enhance our clients' business processes. Agile consulting itself relies extensively on advanced technologies, ranging from SaaS to the latest virtual collaboration tools.

In the remainder of this chapter, we are going to introduce you to some of the technologies we find most helpful to ourselves and to our clients. We will also look at the issue of collaboration and how new tools can support it. But lest you think that we have gone over to the IT dark side, we want to assure you that we are decidedly old-fashioned about how we conduct business at Bluewolf. We may use IT-based collaboration tools, but face-to-face meetings and real-time phone conversations are mandatory, and regarded as the preferred communication option. At the end of the day, the root of the frustration that many executives have with technology is that instead of enhancing communication, the wrong technology sometimes hampers it. And sometimes individuals and organizations have a false sense of security that the technology itself will do the communicating and collaborating, without realizing that the purest form of communication—bar none—happens during direct interaction with another individual, or group of individuals, in the same physical setting.

SaaS

We've previously written quite a bit about SaaS. For businesses, SaaS is a critical technology advance. It allows the business to gain all the benefits of top-notch, proven business software, while avoiding all the complications and drawbacks of custom development and bloated, big-ticket enterprise software packages. Good SaaS products are highly configurable, allowing you to match the software to your particular business process. And the SaaS business model is ideal. It is a subscription model that lets clients know exactly what the software will cost them each month or each year. It can be scaled up or down at will for a predictable price. So, in a nutshell, here are the benefits that we think make SaaS so hugely important:

> **Proven top–notch software:** It offers products that are being used by hundreds or thousands of businesses, and they work as promised the first time.

> **Highly configurable:** You can tweak those products to precisely fit how you do business.

> **Easy to change:** If something about your business changes, it is simple to reconfigure the software.

> **No fuss:** The vendors are constantly enhancing the products, often on a monthly basis; upgrades are transparent to users, and there is no system infrastructure to maintain, just your browser and Internet connection.

> **Low cost:** Not only do you pay a low, predictable subscription fee, but you do not need anywhere the kind of consulting services or IT infrastructure conventional software requires.

> **Mutual efficiency:** SaaS is the most efficient use of computing resources yet invented, and these efficiencies benefit BOTH the vendor and the customer.

It is important to understand why the SaaS model lends itself ideally to customer success. The key to this software breakthrough is its multi-tenant architecture. And without throwing too much credit in one direction, it goes without saying that Salesforce.com has led the charge in defining the pure multi-tenant architecture that is so critical to customer success. It is also worth noting that many so-called SaaS vendors today are NOT multi-tenant.

Multi-tenant is a database, operating system, and application server environment that shares a common data model. For example, in Salesforce.com, there is ONE Customer table, shared by all 30,000 of Salesforce.com's subscribing customers. Merrill Lynch securely stores its Customer Names in the same exact table that your smaller company might. And the entire application works that way. So, at the end of the day, the SaaS vendor does not have to maintain separate environments for each of its customers. It only has to maintain a single environment—albeit a large one—with extensive security built in, to ensure that Merrill Lynch can't see you, and you can't see them.

Compare the multi-tenant architecture to the model that most premise-based software vendors utilize—Microsoft, Oracle, and SAP, for example. In their world, individual customers maintain their own environments, on their choice of hardware and software, and these customer bases are littered with hundreds of version variations that must be supported, and patched, and maintained in their multitude of states. This creates a situation wherein true business process innovation is severely hampered, because the software vendor burns a large chunk of its capital and time writing software for all of these environments.

In a multi-tenant environment, there is only one environment to support. Period. And if the SaaS vendor wants to release a new piece of functionality to help its customers, it only has to write for, and test in, one environment. And if they discover a bug that is affecting their application, they only have to fix it once. This is not a trivial point. In fact, it is the heart of the power of SaaS. Unless you have worked for a software company, or been involved in large-scale, multi-platform software projects, you may not appreciate how difficult it is to make software run properly in hundreds or thousands of different environments.

Oracle, in the 1980s and early 1990s, used to brag about its portability—that is, it could run on hundreds of platforms. But guess what? As a company, Oracle had to maintain separate divisions, organized by platform (i.e. HP, DEC, IBM, TANDEM, etc.), and they had to maintain a wholly separate division—the Porting Division—with hundreds of employees, in order to make that claim. And at the end of the day, who cares? If I am an HP shop, do I benefit from the fact that Oracle spends billions of dollars supporting other platforms? Absolutely not.

There is one additional key to the pure multi-tenant architecture that Salesforce.com brought to market, and, admittedly, it sounds a little creepy. They can see what you are doing. They can see every click of the mouse, every transaction. It sounds awfully Big Brother-esque at first, but it actually works out to be in their clients' best interests. Consider this: Salesforce.com knows which parts of the application get a lot of use, and which ones don't. Instead of having to put together hundreds of mundane focus groups, instead of having to survey their customers incessantly (who ever learns anything really productive from a survey?), the pure SaaS vendor can make deductions regarding the effectiveness of its software simply by watching the actual behavior of its clients through the software itself, much like Amazon.com understands what books to recommend to its consumers. While today we might question how well SaaS vendors are tapping this incredible labyrinth of information, the capacity to do so nonetheless exists.

Ultimately, the power to understand what functions the customer is using—something only SaaS vendors have the ability to do—leads to the cure for the over-engineered software package. And it leads to the end of shelfware, and of overpriced consultants, and never-ending projects. In addition, good SaaS products have growing ecosystems of add-on functionality that can be used to further customize and enhance the software. We have put vertical market-specific functionality for several industries onto Salesforce.com's AppExchange, a marketplace for SFC add-on functionality.

So, call its existence a freak occurrence, but we'll give Salesforce.com and its multi-tenant architecture a nod of gratitude for enabling the agile consulting model we've espoused in this book since page one.

Although not everything we do is SaaS-based, SaaS increasingly plays a role in most of our engagements because it makes so much sense. Without SaaS, companies are at the mercy of the big consulting firms and integrated enterprise application vendors, and most managers already know from painful experience that is a costly dead end.

GUI–Browsers

The intuitive graphical user interface (GUI) and the Internet browser have combined with SaaS to eliminate most of the pain points associated with business software. Specifically, they reduce the end-user learning curve and increase administrator efficiency and productivity. With the GUI and a browser, what might have called for a week or more of end-user training can be reduced to one to two days—or less. Similarly, point-and-click functionality enables administrators to configure and manage the software quickly and easily, no programming required. Some administrators may want to write a few scripts to further automate things, but even that usually isn't necessary.

With point-and-click configuration, you just make the change and go. That means the software can be changed with just a few clicks of the mouse if something in the business changes. Compare that to what you used to have to go through to make even the simplest change—like changing a label on a field—with conventional business software.

The importance of easy GUI-browser technology cannot be overemphasized. Your people already know how to use a browser. They surf the Net, click through Google, and download MP3s to their iPods without missing a beat. They can start clicking their way through your new SaaS application within minutes. You will have to orient them to the application and its new functionality, and familiarize them with security and other procedural issues, but otherwise they are pretty much set to go. Since you have configured the application to support your business processes, employees will find the application natural and intuitive even if the screens aren't the same as before.

We do put a lot of effort into designing and planning the training. However, learning to use GUI-browser technology is nothing like the marathon training sessions people endured to use conventional enterprise software packages. The fact that we start preparing users early in the process streamlines the training even more. Many will already be familiar with early iterations and may have provided input that is reflected in the latest version.

Finally, the ease of learning is instrumental in overcoming resistance to change. As we said previously, there always are people who resist change, often only because they don't want to have to learn the process or the system all over again. Now the new system can be so familiar to begin with, that there is little new to actually learn. Resistance crumbles.

AppExchange

AppExchange is an online marketplace created and maintained by Salesforce.com. AppExchange is where companies using Salesforce.com go to find additional functionality, such as a customization that somebody previously created, and that they're now offering for sale, or even for free. The industry used to call this kind of customization an applet, but that's not quite accurate for AppExchange functionality. AppExchange is sometimes called an on-demand marketplace, because there is no installable software. What that really means is that AppExchange functionality is delivered via the SaaS model too. You can keep your own customizations within your company, or you can make them available to the world at large via AppExchange. However you acquire it, the new functionality runs entirely within your Salesforce.com account at the host, just like the rest of Salesforce.com. In this respect, the AppExchange is a true platform.

The beauty of AppExchange is that it gives you access to incredible amounts of functionality at SaaS pricing (though Bluewolf's aren't, many customizations are even free) and with SaaS ease and convenience. And it ensures that all of your data is stored in one place allowing organizations to avoid the painful task of integrating disparate applications. At the time of this writing, the AppExchange public directory included over 400 applications. By the time you read this, the number will likely be much higher. So you aren't limited to the functionality you originally subscribed to. As your business changes, you can quickly, easily, and cheaply find functionality that addresses those changes, and get it up and running fast. Try doing that with a big licensed enterprise software package.

AppExchange, as it turns out, is just one of the ways you can enhance, alter, or extend functionality. You can use Salesforce.com's regular interface to extend its data schema, you can write custom HTML or JavaScript, work directly with Salesforce.com's API, create your own SQL database calls, use Ajax, and more. Ajax (Asynchronous JavaScript and XML) enables the creation of interactive Web applications. We use Ajax extensively when customizing for our clients.

The real point of this AppExchange discussion is to convey how easy it is to make a SaaS application like Salesforce.com into something that truly matches the particular requirements of your business process. Like the old Burger King ads said, you really can "have it your way." Although this kind of customization is pretty straightforward, and Salesforce.com provides all the tools and guidance to achieve it, most organizations still don't want to be bothered. They want the customization, but prefer to have people like us do it, at least initially. In the process we will still show their people how they can take over for themselves.

This potential to customize SaaS applications illustrates another important trend—the convergence of professional services and technology solutions. In the past, there was a clear distinction between the professional services provided by big consulting companies, and the technology provided by the software vendors. The vendor built, enhanced, and maintained the enterprise application, and the consulting firm helped the client deploy it. Where customization was required, the consulting firm stepped into the application vendor role, and began coding like crazy. That's when you saw the multi-year implementations that cost tens of millions of dollars. Implementation/deployment and customization were two distinct roles. The first consisted of classic professional services; the second clearly fell into the technology product-vendor realm.

SaaS and applications blur this distinction. The 21st century consulting firm must now be prepared to provide and support solutions similar to those of a software vendor, although the vast majority of the code is already there and working. Their customizations may simply involve pointing and clicking through a number of screens to tweak the application so it reflects the client's process exactly. SaaS vendors provide the tools, but they won't do it for you (beyond their regular, ongoing functional enhancements). So the consulting firm steps in, to take responsibility for what was traditionally considered the developer's role. For the professional service firm, the best part of this new arrangement is that it's not that hard anymore, or anywhere near as slow and expensive, to provide these customizations. We knock them out as part of a regular, timeboxed iteration. With a little training, even the client can take over this task.

Why can professional services firms now provide supportable, licensed, solutions? Because SaaS gives us a single platform to work with. In the past, consulting firms delivered solutions across an infinite number of technology stacks, and had to be adept with HP, Sun, IBM, Oracle, Sybase, Informix, Weblogic, WebSphere, Netscape, and more. And each of these stacks came with multiple versions on various point releases, and everything had to be perfectly aligned for any customization to work. So, after building a customization for a client, the last thing that the professional services firm would attempt to do would be to deploy it to and support it for another customer, whose environment was almost guaranteed to be different. Professional services firms understood the madness that companies such as Oracle went through to support their legions of platforms, and so they stuck to the service business.

With SaaS, there is only one platform, and it is always on. Products can be tested and deployed against it easily. So a services firm—which has always been in the best position to truly understand its clients' requirements because it is under contract to understand them—almost has a responsibility to "productize" and support customizations across its customer base. (In the case of consulting, productizing might involve transforming support concepts and techniques, or specific customizations, into a uniquely marketable product.) Otherwise, those firms would be taking code from one account to the next, and charging a time and materials fee to do nothing!

18

Collaboration: The Heart of Agile Consulting

People have probably been collaborating since the first cavemen started using language (if not before!), so the concept isn't exactly new. However, in today's fast moving, global marketplace, where the people who need to be involved are spread across different countries and time zones, collaboration takes on a whole new meaning.

Collaboration becomes especially critical when dealing with business applications. The software does so much and is so complex, that no individual can possibly know everything about it and how it needs to be used. That is why the academics squirreled away on their lush campuses, and divorced from the real world of software users, can't possibly create software that provides practical value in day-to-day operations. They don't know how people might use it, nor do they much care. They intend from the start to create idealized software that they think businesses should want and workers should use. If they collaborated with working people in the real world, they could come up with something of real value. Of course, they have no intention of collaboration, because they feel they know best, and think the rest of us should conform our businesses and work processes to their ideals.

For agile consulting firms, collaboration is built into the process from the start. You can't take the first step, to assemble a success plan, without client collaboration. Any success plan developed without it is meaningless. As defined by the agile consulting success plan, only the particular software users' terms measure success. For example, we know it's true that Salesforce.com works as promised. It does what the vendor says it will do, and probably more, at the price they say. But that isn't success. We can implement it for a client without a hitch, and not even come close to achieving success. We might consolidate the opportunity pipeline, expedite data sharing, eliminate data inconsistency, or do any number of other things, but if those aren't the things the client needs to achieve to be successful, our implementation, regardless of how flawless, is definitely NOT a success. We'll even go so far as to say that success *requires* collaboration.

Our Eighth Law of Consulting Economics says *when it comes to success, communication is everything.* We can now add a critical corollary to that law: Success requires collaboration, which is nothing more than effective communication of the highest order.

Yet another corollary to our Eighth Law is this: The better and deeper the level of collaboration, the greater your chances of achieving success, and of doing it fast. Businesses (or consultants, for that matter) can collaborate halfheartedly. They can choose not to share everything they have learned in the process, or to share it belatedly. They can decide that their success is not integrally tied to the success of the agile team. In short, they can be less than fully engaged players. However, that disengagement will quickly become apparent to everyone else on the team (and they won't be part of any Bluewolf team for long). The iterative agile process quickly exposes what is being accomplished and what is not, and provides the mechanism to identify what is going wrong and why.

Collaboration is built not only into the development of the success plan, but also into every stage of the agile consulting process. The agile team wouldn't even know what to do at any stage in the process if it weren't for the collaborative input it continuously receives. The daily agile team meeting is nothing but a formalized collaboration mechanism. The iterative process is nothing if it isn't collaborative through and through. Knowledge transfer, training, and all other agile processes are built around a communications focus that emphasizes collaboration and more collaboration. Agile consulting, like agile development, is not for lone wolves determined to act as solitary players. Those types of people need to join the potentate-like developers on their leafy campuses. Just in case we haven't made the point clearly enough, collaboration is everything.

So, how do we actually facilitate the collaborative process? The answer is shockingly simple, so much so that it almost sounds stupid just stating it: You collaborate by engaging in an honest dialog with your team members. Do people really need to be told that? You bet. Maybe conversation is a lost art, but dialog is often an overlooked solution. By dialog, we mean interactive, two-way conversation, talking with each other, exchanging ideas, soliciting feedback, asking questions, and answering the questions of others. This kind of dialog goes beyond just reporting the facts or dictating ideas. It requires an honest, open exchange of information and thoughts. The conversations need to be direct and to the point. They can and should be polite and civil. The idea is to communicate everything that needs to be communicated directly and quickly, so team members can accomplish their tasks within the designated timebox.

Our preference always is for face-to-face dialog, although we realize that time and geography don't necessarily allow for that. If face-to-face conversation isn't possible, then we favor telephone calls. Our least favorite communication method is via email. To put it bluntly, in our experience, email sucks. The problems with using email for collaboration are numerous. To begin with, it gets smothered in a sea of spam. You're never really sure if a message got to its destination. The possibility of misunderstanding is great, because there is no emotional dimension to email; it contains none of the verbal and visual signals, the laughs or the looks, that help us fully understand the meaning of the words in face-to-face communication. And those little happy and sad face graphics, like :) or): are a pathetic effort to compensate. Email has its uses. We use it all the time—we couldn't have written this book without email—but for important, collaborative problem-solving, face-to-face or phone communication beats email every time.

Actually, there are some situations where email is necessary, such as for exchanging electronic documents. But even when using email to exchange documents, it is best to precede the exchange with a phone call alerting the recipient that the document is on the way, and to make a follow-up call to confirm that the document has indeed successfully navigated the network, and made its way through the various routers, firewalls, spam filters, and anti-virus defenses. We also find email to be a very effective way to set up in-person and phone meetings (as this book goes to print, the exchange of electronic documents via email is on its last legs. Google's advancements in document storage and sharing is re-shaping collaboration from a document management perspective).

There are some other tools, all Internet-oriented, that also aid this kind of collaborative dialog. They include Google, wikis, blogs, and shared web space.

> **Google:** People know Google first and foremost as a search engine. However, it also provides a set of online applications ranging from email and calendaring, to word processing and spreadsheets. Google does two things that make its tools particularly effective for collaboration:

> 1) Google makes it is easy to share and track whatever you create, particularly with its word processor and spreadsheet.

> 2) Google taps the power of its search engine to make it easy to find information, even if it is buried in complex message threads.

> **Wikis:** Most people know of wikis, which are vehicles for group editing, through Wikipedia—the wildly inaccurate and deservedly much-maligned, much-manipulated "people's encyclopedia." (We don't think Wikipedia is much good for anything more than telling you what the letters of an acronym stand for, and even then you should probably check a second source.) But a collaborative team can create a document, or even complete project documentation, as a wiki—with various team members editing, adding, and deleting information along the way. There are other tools that do this as well. Wikis, however, are pretty intuitive and pretty unstructured, which can be an advantage in many cases.

> **Blogs:** Most people know about blogs through the highly-charged political blogosphere. But at its core, the blog is simply a document or series of documents chronologically presented on the Internet. Links can be embedded in the documents—which appear in the order they were created—and outside comments can be associated with them. Blogs are simple to create, and it is easy to post to them. (Judging

from much of the garbage out in the public blogosphere, it's clear that any idiot can create and post to one.) Like wikis, blogs can be used to document whatever a collaborative team wants to document.

> **Shared webspace:** The Web is full of companies that provide shared online space for a wide range of purposes, from interactive, real-time chat rooms, to shared online storage space. These spaces vary widely in cost (some are free), provide varying degrees of structure (from none to lots of structure), and allow varying degrees of control (again from none to lots of control). They all provide a common online place that all members of a collaborative team can easily get to and participate in.

Around the time we were writing this, Salesforce.com announced its AppSpace. Initially intended as a portal, by the time AppSpace was made public in early spring 2007, it was being positioned as a shared space, more akin to MySpace. Since the early fall of 2006, when Salesforce.com introduced IdeaExchange as a way to capture feedback from customers (aka the SFC community), the company has been even more driven to provide enhancements that customers actually want. Therefore, as part of Salesforce.com's community-driven 22nd release, AppSpace has great potential to aid collaboration. Compare that to how the software academics build applications off in their ivory towers.

All of these communication and collaboration options are valuable to a certain extent. Still, they only augment the collaboration and dialog that must be at the heart of every agile consulting engagement. They cannot replace face-to-face meetings and real-time, live conversation.

The upshot is that dialog is an ongoing component of every agile consulting engagement, from the first contact to the final sign-off. And even then, the dialog should never stop, since the business and the market continually changes. These changes may necessitate yet another iteration, or maybe an entirely new engagement. And the only way to know that is to keep the conversation going.

19
Driving Adoption

No matter how swimmingly an IT project has theoretically gone, the true test of success for the client lies in driving adoption. Regardless of whether a business pays nine figures or three to get the functionality it needs, if its workers don't use the software appropriately, it is worth nothing. Successful implementation's provide working software that delivers business value every day—in other words, the absolute antithesis of shelfware. That is why driving adoption is so critical to success.

Remember the mantra in the movie *Field of Dreams*, "If you build it, he will come"? Sorry, but that doesn't happen with business software. (In the rare case you've gotten lucky in this regard, consider it a gift from God.) Software adoption doesn't just happen out of the blue; even a switch to the best, most intuitive software involves embracing change—something people have a tendency to resist, even when that change is good. The old software could have been a widely acknowledged disaster, something that seemingly everybody loathed. It could have been cumbersome to the nth degree, or been frustratingly slow. It could have been unreliable, and prone to frequent crashes. It could have been any or all of these things, and still some people would resist its replacement. It doesn't matter if the new software is intuitive and easy to use, something any 5-year-old or even a CEO could handle. Even software loaded with the users' wish lists of every feature and function they've asked for—a veritable Santa's list of treats for good boys and girls—will meet resistance from some.

This brings us to our *Fourteenth Law of Consulting Economics: There is no ROI on business software without widespread user adoption.* That's right, no ROI—zero, nada, zilch, nothing—because if users don't adopt the software on a broad scale, you don't get any benefit or payback worth counting. You can't count on users to automatically adopt new software; you've got to make it happen.

We take the adoption strategy further than most consultants, striving for what we refer to as "adoption to addiction." We strive to get to the point where people won't want to function *without* your software. Unlike other consulting firms, we start working on adoption on day one, building it into the success plan from the start. There are six parts to our "adoption to addiction" program:

> **Early start;**
> **User involvement;**
> **Communications;**
> **Change management;**
> **Training materials;**
> **Phased deployment.**

Let's look at each one. We've mentioned the early start. This involves more than just building adoption efforts into the success plan. It means defining adoption success criteria and figuring out how to measure them. It also involves preparing a curriculum and writing test plans.

User involvement is just what it seems to be. Adoption results from giving the users what they need, in a way they can use it. There's no way to know what the users really need or how they are going to work with the software, without putting some of them on the team. Ultimately, to achieve successful adoption, the users must embrace the software as their own, built for them and by them.

Communications really means no surprises. Consultants need to start communicating with users from the start about what they want to do, how they are going to go about it, and why the users will want it. It requires soliciting user input from the start and actually hearing and acting upon what they say. Our Eighth Law of Consulting Economics says that communication is everything. It applies to adoption as much as it does to every other aspect of agile consulting.

At another level, communication is about selling. Even if users hate the existing system, they generally hate change even more. Consultants need to sell users on the necessity of change from the existing system. They can do that by communicating the benefits users will experience by participating in the change process, and ultimately making the switch. As they begin to demonstrate early iterations of the new system, their communications effort has to involve spreading the word—in users' terms— about how much of an improvement the new software really is. Ideally, members of other departments will be clamoring to be the next in line for the new software.

Change management entails understanding the nature of change, and managing its pace. As we said before, there should be no surprises. Consultants and the client must communicate well, and pay attention to the feedback they receive. When problems come up, they have to be addressed fast, and everybody involved needs to know they have been addressed. Other elements of change management include quarterly reviews, the development of centers of excellence to support the system and its users, and application governance.

Training materials can take many forms: documentation, help files, self-paced tutorials, hands-on demos, instructor-led training, on-demand learning, and more. Which options to use depend on the software, the users, and their attitudes toward learning.

Finally, we typically favor phased deployment, rather than a "Big Bang" deployment. We build success with each group that deploys the software, and the interest and anticipation builds. It also gives us the opportunity to fine-tune the training and deployment process as we go; it amounts to iterative training and deployment.

In fact, phased deployments should never end. Rather, they should morph into continuous education. With iterative software, you are always enhancing the system because your business and your market keep changing. By making continuous education part of an ongoing deployment process, you can avoid the costly and disruptive changes that occur when companies find themselves faced with a forklift upgrade to a new system (a change they have put off too long, because of the disruption it would likely cause).

If you have been following agile consulting practices, it is not hard to drive adoption to addiction. Much of what you need to do—like ensure user involvement, change management, and communication—is built into the process anyway. The users who have been part of the development effort from the start will naturally become evangelists for the resulting software, which will further smooth the effort. And you certainly won't have any fear that your efforts will result in shelfware. With the agile consulting process, it is impossible to create shelfware (unless you deliberately try to). In the end, change management may be the biggest challenge when it comes to adoption. We work extensively with our clients on change management. The next chapter captures how we do it.

20
Managing Change

How important is managing change? In a 2001 report entitled "CRM: The Workers Own the Means of Production," Gartner analyst Jennifer Kirkby wrote, "Leaving behavior unchanged or changing it the wrong way is often the cause of CRM failure." This is a pretty scary statement for us, because we often work on CRM initiatives, and more importantly, for our customers who are spending real money on CRM and don't like to even consider the possibility of failure. (We don't either; we've designed the agile consulting methodology to identify potential failures early in the process and mitigate them on the spot. We've also built in change management throughout the entire process.)

So what do we mean by change management? Here's the fancy consulting company definition: Change management is a proactive approach to identifying and managing behavioral and organization factors that impact the outcome of an initiative. We actually think of it a little bit differently: Change management helps us to ensure that our customers meet their business objectives. The objectives can be performance goals, success criteria from our success plan, or something else that gives the client a competitive advantage. In terms of software, change management is a process that focuses on meeting end-user needs during the transition from one software application, to the new application that will supersede it. The objective of change management, as far as we're concerned, is to drive user adoption of the new system. By the way, change management isn't a one-time thing. Once the users have adopted the software and the client signs off on the success plan and sends us packing, change management must continue, because the applications, business, and users will continually change. In order to keep on top of those changes and address whatever issues arise, change management remains necessary.

You already know we are not great fans of technology for technology's sake. In part, that's because in the past, in regard to software and technology, the words "change management" were considered dirty ones. Any attention to technology was paid only to ensure that it worked. (That it often didn't work as promised or even as expected didn't seem to bother a lot of people, including the clients.) Clients and consultants simply assumed that all they had to do was run a few training courses so users would adopt the software, and wonderful results would follow. That didn't usually happen, which shouldn't surprise anyone.

In 2000, a venture capital firm did a study suggesting that the technology aspect of any software project only accounted for 15% of the adoption problem. Can you guess what the critical issue was? It was managing people through the transition to new software. In the SaaS world, where the underlying technology actually plays a miniscule role—far less than 15%, no doubt—the challenge is people, not technology. The key challenges, then, are change and process management. But adoption is critical. It doesn't matter if we meet the success factors that we defined with the client—what's the point if nobody uses the software? For that matter, if nobody is using the software, how can we say we've even met those success factors at all? It's like the old question about whether a tree falling in the forest makes a sound if nobody is there to hear it. If nobody is using the software, it doesn't matter what the software can do. It's not *doing* anything.

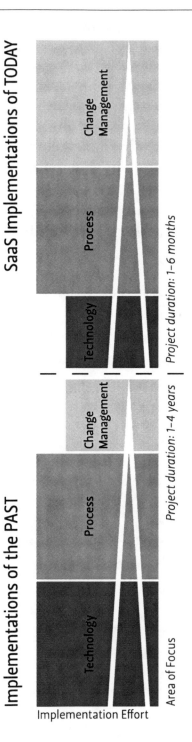

This graphic captures exactly the change that has occurred since the advent of SaaS, in terms of technology and change management. Before SaaS, technology and process management commanded the bulk of the focus and attention, and projects lasted as long as four years. Change management was an afterthought. In the SaaS era, technology is a small concern at the outset. Process and change management command the bulk of the attention, and the projects last six months, max.

A 2002 Deloitte & Touche study of CIOs came to a conclusion similar to that of the North Point Software Venture report. It found that six out of ten barriers to business transformation were people-related. So, what are these people-related factors? Here's the list; you might have others you can add:

> - **Resistance by employees;**
> - **Inadequate sponsorship;**
> - **Unrealistic expectations;**
> - **A poorly-compelling business case;**
> - **A project team lacking in the necessary skills;**
> - **No organizational change plan.**

Change management addresses all of these shortcomings, along with any other people-related factors. Specifically, change management as we envision it can do six important things:

1. **Minimize the transition's impact on the client's employee performance;**
2. **Identify and address risks to achieving the client's success criteria;**
3. **Position the initiative to properly support the client's business objectives;**
4. **Determine the appropriate metrics to begin measuring ROI;**
5. **Develop a customized communications plan to fit the client's corporate culture;**
6. **Accelerate the learning curve through tailored education.**

The result of these change management initiatives is an accelerated adoption of the SaaS implementation. In addition, we have developed a five-stage adoption process that involves analysis, design, implementation, support, and improvement. The graphic below illustrates the process linearly. Don't take it literally—it's actually a continuous cycle.

User Adoption Cycle

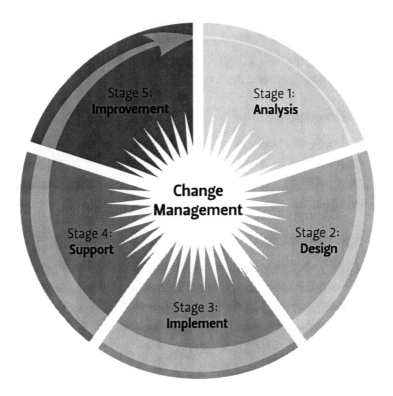

Here is the process in a bit more detail:

Stage 1: Analysis

Assess the readiness of the end-users through discovery phase interviews. Make sure to meet with a cross representation of end-users.

Stage 2: Design

Design systems and curricula that meet the end-users' true day-in-the-life experiences. To ensure they won't merely be attending product training, make sure to include real business process training that provides best practices that have proven successful.

Stage 3: Implement

Launch the system, support structures, and training domestically and internationally. We prefer to do it in phases by business unit or geography. (Remember our metaphor of trying to teach 1000 people to dance versus trying to teach a few small groups? After you have a few groups doing the dance, they will help teach the others.)

Stage 4: Support

Design a support structure that best fits the client's corporate culture. (We also take a look at creating a baseline and coaching them on how to assess their ROI by doing 3-month, 6-month, 9-month, and one-year assessments.)

Stage 5: Improvement

Strategically plan how to improve not only the system itself, but its utilization by the end-users. Are they ready for more advanced features? Can the system's capabilities be increased to meet the needs of the organization so that it can sustain the company's growth?

Remember: Change Management isn't a once-through linear process; it is cyclical, and continuous.

21
Conclusion: Avoiding Disintermediation

Remember the term disintermediation? That long, ugly word essentially means the process of eliminating some kind of intermediary in a value chain. The advent of e-commerce made it possible to eliminate plenty of middlemen—whether individuals or businesses—that once added modest amounts of value along the supply chain. Online banking and ATMs, for example disintermediated a lot of live tellers. Travel websites disintermediated an entire segment of retail travel agents. The few that survived somehow managed to reinvent themselves as corporate travel logistics organizations, or discount consumer travel packagers. Of course, disintermediation isn't new. We guess that when it came to overland transportation, for example, you could say that the automobile disintermediated the horse, and gas stations disintermediated animal feed suppliers. With the Internet and the new, fast-paced global economy, however, the speed of disintermediation and the breadth of intermediaries susceptible to it have greatly increased.

Now, the combination of agile consulting, the Internet, and SaaS threaten to disintermediate the conventional business software consulting firms that actually survived the dotcom collapse and the economic down-turn that followed. Of course, many of those that are still around don't really play in the business software arena anymore. Some have become infrastructure companies. Others have gone into the offshore outsourcing business by opening development centers in places where they can play the IT-labor wage-arbitrage game. The problem for conventional business software consulting firms is that the kind of bread-and-butter work that made consulting so much fun—the big seven-, eight-, and even nine-fig-ure, multi-year engagements, with no pressure to deliver actual results—has disappeared. Today, even managers at the most dinosaur-like corpora-tions, who are accustomed to overpaying for systems and software, are demanding deliverables in 30 to 90 days, and resisting price tags higher than a few hundred grand. Now that their clients are discerning about the prices they are willing to pay, the old-school IT consulting firms are going to have to set their consultants up with little collection buckets on street corners, like the Salvation Army at Christmas—if they plan to keep them on the street at all. Even these consultants' favored software products—systems like Siebel and Peoplesoft—are going the way of the dinosaurs, as the enterprise packaged software industry consolidates, and vendors like Oracle and SAP forego innovation to become the computer associates and IBM's of yesteryear. History *does* repeat itself.

The old consulting business model has long been ripe for disintermedi-ation. That it lasted as long as it did is a testament to the human tendency to resist change, something we've highlighted in our previous discussion about driving adoption and change management. Even seemingly smart corporate executives have difficulty bucking ingrained habits. If a com-pany needs new software functionality because its business or market is changing right under its feet, the inbred habit is to call a big conventional software consulting company. As predictable as filing taxes on April 15th, they will recommend sending in a few dozen consultants to do a gap analysis and come up with recommendations, etc., etc., etc. You already know the story. That's one reason, we hope, why you've read our book this far. (Relax, we're almost at the end.)

Well, corporate executives have experienced enough pain, and they are finally getting smart. They know that the world definitely has changed. They finally recognize that the old way of doing business, the way they did it in 1970, and 1980, and 1990, cannot be the way they do business in the 21st century—at least not if they want their stock options and golden parachutes to be worth anything when they move on or retire. As comfortable as the old ways of doing things were, they just won't cut it anymore. Those traditional consulting firms have been disintermediated, whether they realize it or not.

Of course, the more astute conventional consulting executives have seen the proverbial handwriting on the wall. They know the game is coming to an end sooner rather than later, and have taken steps to reinvent themselves. A few others will simply try to play out the game for as long as they can, in the hope that it will take them to a point where they can comfortably retire. Maybe there will even be some value in a diminishing client list they can sell to someone else. (Heck, for the right price maybe we'd even buy those client relationships, and try to convert them to the agile consulting approach!) A few others may have reached the point where they have enough clients on annual support contracts (think of it as lifetime consultant support) that they can simply cruise to retirement on the annuities they bring in.

The future, if you haven't guessed by now, lies in agile consulting for agile businesses, because change—fast, frequent, unexpected, and often dramatic—is a given. If your business isn't agile and you don't want it to become so, then you won't have a chance of being able to cope with the kind of change that is occurring now, and is sure to continue in the future. Your business simply won't have much of a future. Thank you for buying this book, but it probably won't help you much.

The future lies with companies that want to be agile, that are willing to change as their customers and markets change, and are attempting to adapt their processes and systems to the new reality, whatever that may be. And if that reality shifts again in three months, six months, twenty-four months, or whenever, they are willing and able to make the necessary changes once again. If they don't, well, they won't be the first company to become extinct. So, let's make this the fifteenth and final Law of Consulting Economics: *Expect change.* That means everything will change; you, your business, your clients, their businesses, the market, technology, everything. Be ready to change and change again, as often as necessary. Some people find this distressing. We find it exhilarating. If we had a corollary to this it would be our Third Law, iterate or die.

It sounds harsh but that's the sad, hard truth. Free market capitalism, which is sweeping the world (in case you haven't noticed, just look at so-called Communist China), is driven by the kind of creative destruction spawned by free market capitalism and the entrepreneurism it spawns. Only by destroying the existing, aging economic models and leaders can new and better models emerge. Agile consulting, in that sense, is just another example of creative destruction. It is already in the process of destroying the conventional business software consulting model. Of course, our hope is that embedded into the agile consulting model is its own capacity to sense the next wave of creative destruction, and the dynamic ability and adjust to that, too. The imperative of change is to iterate or die. We don't intend to die as a business, and hope you don't either.

Citations

Chapter 1

McKenna, Christopher. *The World's Newest Profession: Management Consulting in the Twentieth Century*. New York: Cambridge University Press, 2006.

Chapter 2

McKenna, Christopher. *The World's Newest Profession: Management Consulting in the Twentieth Century*. New York: Cambridge University Press, 2006.

Freeland, John, Ed. *The Ultimate CRM Handbook: Strategies and Concepts for Building Enduring Customer Loyalty and Profitability*. New York: McGraw Hill. 2003.

Greenberg, Paul. *CRM at the Speed of Light: Essential Customer Strategies for the 21st Century*. New York: McGraw Hill/Osborne, 2004.

Chapter 3

Andres Gillies. "Stock Focus: Internet Consulting Companies," *Forbes* magazine, Oct. 2000, http://www.forbes.com/2000/10/19/1019sf.html

Chapter 4

Beck, Kent. *Extreme Programming Explained: Embrace Change*. Boston: Addison-Wesley, 2000.

Weintraub, Alan and Logan, Debra. *An IDM Project: From Strategic Plan to Implementation Plan*. The Gartner Group, October 10, 2000

Larman, Craig. *Agile & Iterative Development: A Manager's Guide*. Boston: Addison-Wesley, 2004.

Chapter 8

Hammer, Michael and James Champy. *Reengineering the Corporation: A Manifesto for Business Revolution*. New York: HarperBusiness Essentials, 2003.

Chapter 10

Saracevic, Alan T. and Benjamin Pimentel, Dan Fost, Vern Kopytoff, Jessica Guynn and Colleen Benson, "On the Record: Marc Benioff," *San Francisco Chronicle,* October 8, 2006, C-1

Chapter 11

McGee, Marianne Kolbasuk. "With the H-1B Visa Cap Filled in Record Time, Reform is in the Air," *Information Week,* 9 April 2007, 29.

Chapter 13

Larman, Craig. *Agile & Iterative Development: A Manager's Guide.* Boston: Addison-Wesley, 2004.

Chapter 14

Larman, Craig. *Agile & Iterative Development: A Manager's Guide.* Boston: Addison-Wesley, 2004.

Chapter 20

Kirkby, Jennifer. "CRM: The Workers Own the Means of Production." Gartner Inc, Stamford, CT, 2001.

Appendix A:
Bluewolf Laws of Consulting Economics

1. *Projects don't matter, results matter.*

2. *A successful business process trumps cool technology.*

3. *Iterate or die.*

4. *Outsourcing is not consulting.*

5. *Make agile methodology the consulting practice model.*

6. *Throw out the rules.*

7. *When facing quicksand, steer clear of it.*

8. *When it comes to success, communication is everything.*

9. *Do not rely on the Great Man for project salvation.*

10. *Full project transparency avoids surprises.*

11. *Every project must start with a specific success plan.*

12. *Play to your strengths.*

13. *Be ready and willing to fight hard (and fairly) for what you feel is best.*

14. *There is no ROI on business software without widespread user adoption.*

15. *Expect change.*

Appendix B:
Glossary

Agile business—An organization culturally and operationally prepared to respond quickly to changes in the market.

Agile consulting—A consulting methodology that uses an iterative approach to problem solving and solution development, and promotes the quick delivery of business value. The agile approach is Bluewolf's guiding consulting philosophy.

Agile development—A set of programming techniques and methodologies that employ iterative approaches to deliver software functionality quickly.

AppExchange—A marketplace managed by Saleforce.com (SFC) to showcase and provide third-party additions to SFC core functionality.

AppSpace—A two-way team collaboration portal for business, hosted and managed by SFC, and linked to both SFC's core product and AppExchange.

Application service provider (ASP)—A third party that hosts and runs applications for clients on a fee basis, and a forerunner of SaaS.

Blog—The short form of "weblog," a blog is a Web or intranet site on which a single user or group of people publish chronological content (usually commentary or narrative). The blog creator will often allow others to post comments on (or less commonly, to edit) the content. Blog also refers to the action of posting updates to the site.

Business Process Outsourcing (BPO)—The outsourcing of complete business operational functions, such as AR/AP, to a third-party; usually reserved for non-strategic business processes and functions.

Chief Information Officer (CIO)—The organization's top manager with direct responsibility for IT planning and strategy, and IT operations.

Chief Process Officer (CPO)—The organization's top manager with a direct mandate to optimize, redesign, and manage the organization's business processes across all business units and vertical silos.

Customer Relationship Management (CRM)—Software that helps the organization monitor and manage its relationships with customers, for the purpose of maximizing the business value of the relationship and improving customer service.

Database Administrator (DBA)—An IT person charged with deploying and managing the organization's production databases.

Disintermediation—The elimination of intermediaries in a business process or value chain through the redesign of business processes, and enabled by new capabilities or new technologies.

Enterprise Resource Planning (ERP)—Complex, integrated, company-wide software used to manage core production processes; the broader successor to MRP and MRP II systems.

Extreme programming (XP)—One of a number of agile development methodologies that feature fast iterations, collaborative teams, and pair coding.

Graphical User Interface (GUI)—A visual interface characterized by easy-to-use drop- down menus, dialog boxes, and point-and-click and drag-and-drop functionality, as found in Web browsers or Windows and Apple interfaces.

Iterative—Describes a change process characterized by short, incremental steps or phases.

Iterate—The act of making changes fast.

Managed Service Provider (MSP)—A provider of hosted infrastructure services, such as network management.

Offshoring—The contracting of resource providers overseas, in order to take advantage of the lower cost of labor in the offshore location.

Outsourcing—The act of turning over tasks or processes previously handled in-house to outside providers, which may be onshore or offshore.

Return on Investment (ROI)—A ratio expressing the value of a benefit received, in comparison with the investment required to achieve that benefit.

Software-as-a-Service (SaaS)—Software provided by a third-party as a service delivered over a network, either on a subscription or metered basis.

Salesforce.com (SFC)—The industry-leading CRM software provider that pioneered the SaaS industry.

Service-oriented Architecture (SOA)—A technology architecture for providing IT and business functionality as a reusable service.

Success plan—A document that describes the business value expected from a project, and the various steps that constitute it, along with metrics for determining if, when, and to what extent the expected value has been received. The success plan is central to Bluewolf's agile consulting process.

Timebox—A fixed time period, usually not longer than 90 days, during which a specific deliverable must be completed. The time period does not change, but the scope of the deliverable may change to fit within the fixed period.

Total Cost of Ownership (TCO)—The cost of an acquisition, usually a technology acquisition, plus the cost of deploying, maintaining, and supporting that acquisition through its life. Recently, the cost of disposal has been added to TCO calculations.

Venture capital (VC)—Funding provided by outside investors to underwrite new ventures. The goal is to sell the new venture or to take it public (another form of selling it) to produce a very high return.

Waterfall methodology—An approach to project development that calls for the requirements of the project to be fully analyzed and documented at the outset. The requirements are then forwarded to the development team for implementation. This approach does not easily accommodate change.

Wiki—A form of collaborative document creation, editing, and ongoing revision.

Year 2000 (Y2K)—Shorthand for the problems anticipated when computer systems operating with a two-digit year designation reverted back to 00 in the year 2000. (Few problems actually materialized.)

Appendix C:
IT Salary Guide (2008)

Information technology professionals in the United States can expect starting salaries in 2008 to increase an average of 2.7 percent over 2007.

The following is a comprehensive report of projected salary ranges for the upcoming year. Our predictions are based on the trends we have seen in the past, and that we continue to watch into 2008. Investments in several key areas, including network security, business intelligence, wireless communications, and web applications have and will continue to drive aggressive hiring.

Additionally, figures from the Bureau of Labor Statistics indicate that companies are creating new IT jobs as fast as, or faster than, they can export them overseas. These trends will clearly lead to a rise in demand for IT professionals in the United States, and will result in a significant increase in the average salary.

Using our data of salary growth over the past few years, we have put together a table of projected annual salary ranges for 2008 in the areas of Administration, Application Development, Consulting and Systems Integration, Data and Database Administration, Quality Assurance and Testing, Internet and E-Commerce, Networking and Telecommunications, Security, Software Development, and Technical Services including Help Desk and Technical Support.

Our calculations have found that those working in the areas of Application Development and Systems Integration will enjoy the greatest salary gains in 2008. Their base compensation is expected to rise 4.1 percent and 5.9 percent respectively, bringing Application Development salaries to between $57,500 and $112,500 and Systems Integration salaries to between $70,100 and $134,500.

It is important to note that with the majority of our experience being in the New York area, our numbers may appear inflated when held against a national average. Salary ranges tend to be approximately 25 percent higher in the Northeast and on the West Coast, while rising to approximately 150 percent in the New York Area.

Key findings:

> - **Project managers will earn an average starting salary of between $72,750 and $106,250 annually, an increase of 4.1 percent from 2006.**
> - **Quality assurance analysts can expect base compensation between $52,250 and $74,500, a gain of 4.1 percent.**
> - **Application architects will see starting salaries rise 4 percent, to between $80,000 and $112,750.**
> - **Base compensation for network security administrators will increase 3.7 percent, with starting salaries of between $69,750 and $98,500.**
> - **Average starting salaries for IT auditors will rise 3.1 percent, to between $69,250 and $97,000.**

ADMINISTRATION

Chief Information Officer	$115,000 – $200,000
Chief Technology Officer	$98,000 – $160,000
Vice President of Information Technology	$105,000 – $155,000
Information–Technology Manager	$90,000 – $115,000

APPLICATIONS DEVELOPMENT

Systems Analyst	$65,000 – $90,000
Applications Architect	$80,000 – $110,000
Business Analyst	$65,000 – $90,000
Developer/Program Analyst	$55,000 – $93,000
Lead Applications Developer	$75,000 – $100,000

CONSULTING AND SYSTEMS INTEGRATION

Director	$90,000 – $150,000
Project Manager/Senior Consultant	$75,000 – $130,000
InformationTechnology Auditor	$70,000 – $110,000

DATA/DATABASE ADMINISTRATION

Database Developer	$70,000 – $105,000
Database Administration	$70,000 – $115,000
Data Architect	$85,000 – $110,000
Data Modeler	$80,000 – $120,000
Data–Warehouse Analyst	$75,000 – $110,000
Business–Intelligence Analyst	$70,000 – $100,000

ERP

Technical Analyst	$90,000 – $115,000
Techno–Functional Analyst	$95,000 – $125,000
Functional Analyst	$100,000 – $130,000

QUALITY ASSURANCE AND TESTING

Quality–Assurance Analyst/Tester	$55,000 – $75,000

INTERNET AND E–COMMERCE

Senior Web Developer	$70,000 – $100,000
Web Developer	$55,000 – $75,000
Web Designer	$45,000 – $80,000
E–Commerce Analyst	$65,000 – $85,000

NETWORKING/TELECOMMUNICATIONS

Network Administrator	$65,000 – $95,000
Network Manager	$70,000 – $90,000
Network Engineer	$70,000 – $95,000
Network Administrator	$45,000 – $71,000

SOFTWARE DEVELOPMENT

Product Manager	$75,000 – $105,000
Software Engineer	$75,000 – $100,000
Software Developer	$60,000 – $90,000

TECHNICAL SERVICES, HELP DESK AND TECHNICAL SUPPORT

Desktop–Support Analyst	$45,000 – $65,000
Systems Administrator	$50,000 – $80,000
Help Desk (top–tier)	$45,000 – $55,000
Interactive Producer	$75,000 – $100,000
Information Architect	$85,000 – $110,000

Appendix D:
IT Hiring Tips

Proven Hiring Tips

Make Your Decision Swiftly

Why? Because almost every person you interview will have multiple interviews running at the same time. Speed matters when deciding if a candidate fits your requirements; even more so if the job requires, and they possess, certain high demand skill sets.

Signing Bonuses are Back

Why? They're a great way to tip the scales in your favor, and show a candidate how valuable they are to you.

Be Open to Virtual Offices

Why? The concerns of telecommuting are long past. Be flexible— allowing a person to work 1 to 2 days from a home office will make your offer more competitive.

Offer a Competitive Salary

Why? Salaries are rising every day, especially for those skilled in the highest demand areas, such as all Oracle Technologies, .NET, C#, Flash, and Information Architects.

If you are not prepared to offer a competitive salary, you will not land your candidate of choice.

Don't Set Up More than Two Face-to-Face Interviews

Why? Candidates expect a decision without having to return for a third interview.

Use Fifteen Minute Phone Screens

Why? It saves a lot of time and gives your recruiter or HR department the ability to gather important intelligence about the soft skills necessary for a good fit.

Sponsor an H1B Visa

Why? Your candidate pool can sometimes increase by 500% if your company is open to H1B sponsorship. Typically, the total filing and legal fees are less than $5,000 per transaction, and the process takes less than one day to complete.

Show the Candidate How Working at Your Company Will Enable Them to Learn New Technologies

Why? Technology candidates are interested in expanding their knowledge base, and want to know that their employer will support their career development.

Hire for Today's Need and Tomorrow's Vision

Why? Remember that you're hiring for the future. New people should provide the skills you need in the future, not just match the job demands you see today. Be clear about your strategic direction for the future, and then hire the talent to help you achieve it.

Appendix E:
Sample Success Plan

This was an actual success plan for a real client, designated here as XYZ.

Bluewolf Success Guarantee

Bluewolf is committed to the success of its customers and their roll out and use of Salesforce.com. In order to ensure XYZ's success, Bluewolf provided a Success Guarantee based on specific criteria identified in the requirements sessions. Per this arrangement, the final 10% of fees were to be paid upon XYZ's achievement of the Success Criteria milestones (Bluewolf Success Guarantee) defined in this document. The Success Criteria identified below would have been determined, and must have been agreed upon by both parties during the requirements phase.

Requirements Meetings

XYZ's Success Plan is dependent on the completion of all requirements sessions. The following table captures all critical meetings to be completed and is the basis for this Success Plan, and ultimately for the Bluewolf Success Guarantee.

Name	Date Started	Date Completed	Notes
Kick-off Presentation			
General BPR Session			
GRH and AA BPR Sessions			
APR Session			

TPR Session			
BPR Notes			
APR Document			
TPR Document			

Success Criteria Definitions

Several factors are required to create a single success criterion. This section describes the information required for each field in the Success Criteria.

ID	Description
Goal	Describes the high-level objective.
Situation Assessment	Describes in detail the current state of the issue, including pain points, desired results and ancillary details.
Proposed Solution	Bluewolf's proposal for meeting the goal to resolve the issue.
Success Criteria	Results to be measured at the completion of the project.
Bluewolf Responsibilities	Bluewolf's responsibilities for meeting the Success Criteria.
XYZ Responsibilities	XYZ's responsibilities for meeting the Success Criteria.
Evaluation	Analyses of success (roughly 4 weeks after rollout).

Success Criteria #1

ID	Description
Goal	**Achieve an efficient case management process.** [Applies to Association Affinity (AA) and Group Retiree Health (GRH) Users]

Situation Assessment	XYZ AA users currently utilize a Lotus Notes system to manage case information. The case essentially encompasses the process by which XYZ tracks new or renewal business, and manages the associated tasks related to the case. The case originates either as a Request for Proposal (RFP) or an acquired book of business. During the Sales and/or proposal process, Hartford personnel in various departments need to be involved with a particular case. It is crucial to XYZ that as the case progresses through the process, the appropriate personnel are notified and tasked with their respective "to do" items. These "to do" or diary items need to be assigned to the appropriate personnel and must contain an accurate due date, in order for the process to move smoothly from one step to the next. The GRH group currently lacks a formal system to manage their cases. It is XYZ's desire to have both AA and GRH manage cases in a single system.
Proposed Solution	XYZ will leverage Salesforce.com as the platform to build their Case Management Solution. The base system will be configured to capture the required data elements as well as support their business processes. The custom application will contain a GUI interface that has a tab interface for page layout efficiency. A custom search capability will be developed to filter various lookup fields. The custom GUI will also accommodate field dependencies that cannot be configured through native Salesforce functionality.
Success Criteria	Users will be able to easily create and edit cases via a custom- developed interface that will support their data requirements along with their business process.

Bluewolf Responsibilities	1. Configure custom fields in Salesforce.com to capture Case Management Data.
	2. Develop custom sControls for the following screens:
	a. Pre–Sale
	b. Sold Case
	c. Renewal
	d. Request for Change
	e. Global Request for Change
	3. Use record types to control the views for each business unit.
	4. Provide functional specification documents for each of the sControls.
XYZ Responsibilities	1. Provide the necessary data elements and their relationships to Bluewolf at the beginning of each sprint.
	2. Freeze feature requests at the beginning of each sprint. Move any additional or changed features realized while a sprint is in progress to the Product Backlog.
	3. Effectively communicate the functional and technical requirements to Bluewolf.
	4. Review and approve all related documentation provided by Bluewolf that supports the development of the solution.
Evaluation	Analysis of success (roughly 4 weeks after rollout).

Success Criteria #2

ID	Description
Goal	**Achieve a single repository for case–related information.** (Applies to Association Affinity and Group Retiree Health Users)
Situation Assessment	XYZ's AA and GRH groups currently use disparate systems to manage their case–related information.

Proposed Solution	Upon going live, case-related information would be entered into Salesforce through a custom case management screen. Bluewolf will work with XYZ, providing advice on compiling and de-duplicating the existing data. Bluewolf will migrate the existing case records. Bluewolf and XYZ will define what data will be migrated. The specific tasks and milestones will be further detailed in the Data Migration Plan.
Success Criteria	1. Salesforce becomes the system of record for all case related data. 2. Users will have one system to go to in order to get case-related information. The status of any particular case will be identified, along with the next steps that should be taken.
Bluewolf Responsibilities	1. Configure Salesforce.com case and related objects to capture required data elements. 2. Modify standard and/or create custom reports utilizing out- of-the-box functionality only. 3. Provide XYZ with templates for loading data. 4. Train XYZ staff on the necessary Salesforce.com concepts, enabling them to manage their system independently.
XYZ Responsibilities	1. Provide business and technical resources to compile and de-duplicate records. 2. Freeze feature requests at the beginning of each sprint. Move any additional or changed features realized while a sprint is in progress to the Product Backlog. 3. Provide business and technical resources to link cases to the appropriate Account and Contact records. 4. Assume responsibility for the execution of the data cleansing effort. 5. Provide examples of existing reports or specifications of data that XYZ desires its own reports to reflect. 6. Commit the time necessary to understand how to run reports in Salesforce, at least five business days before BAT of sprint #2.
Evaluation	Analysis of success (roughly 4 weeks after rollout).

ID	Description
Goal	**Achieve a single repository for Account and Contact information.** (Applies to Association Affinity and Group Retiree Health Users)
Situation Assessment	XYZ's AA and GRH groups currently use disparate systems to manage their Customer, Producer, and Third Party Administrator information. In Salesforce, this terminology is broken down into two distinct entities. Accounts (companies with whom they do business, customers, producers, administrators) and Contacts (individuals who work for those companies).
Proposed Solution	Upon going live, all Account- and Contact-related information will be entered into Salesforce using the standard functionality provided by the system. Bluewolf will work with XYZ, providing advice on compiling and de-duplicating the existing data. Bluewolf will migrate the existing Account and Contact records. Bluewolf and XYZ will define what data will be migrated. The specific tasks and milestones will be further detailed in the Data Migration Plan.
Success Criteria	Salesforce becomes the system of record for all Account and Contact data. Users will have one system to go to in order to get information about a specific company or individual they do business with. Comprehensive Account and Contact reporting can be accomplished through Salesforce.com.
Bluewolf Responsibilities	1. Configure fields on Salesforce Account and Contact objects to capture the required data elements. 2. Modify standard-functionality-SFDC reports per XYZ's requirements. 3. Configure an add-in App-exchange module (to be purchased by XYZ, to handle reporting that cannot be achieved using the SFDC Reporting application. 4. Provide XYZ with templates for loading data. 5. Provide XYZ with a Data Migration Plan document. 6. Train XYZ staff on the necessary Salesforce.com concepts, enabling them to manage their system independently.

XYZ Responsibilities	1. Provide business and technical resources to compile and de-duplicate records.
	2. Freeze feature requests at the beginning of each sprint. Move any additional or changed features realized while a sprint is in progress to the Product Backlog.
	3. Provide business and technical resources to link contact records to accounts.
	4. Commit the time necessary to understand how to run reports in Salesforce.
Evaluation	Analysis of success (roughly 4 weeks after rollout).

Success Criteria # 4

ID	Description
Goal	**Achieve sold case integration with Salesforce.com.** (Applies to Association Affinity and Group Retiree Health Users)
Situation Assessment	The integration requirement is a one-way push of case-related data from Salesforce.com to XYZ's sold case system.
Proposed Solution	Utilizing Bluewolf's Enterprise Salesforce Integration (ESI) product sold case data can be pushed from Salesforce.com to XYZ's Sold Case system.
Success Criteria	Relevant case data managed in Salesforce.com will be integrated with XYZ's Sold Case system. Information from Salesforce.com will be pushed downstream to Sold Case based upon status and/or other criteria defined by XYZ.
Bluewolf Responsibilities	1. Installation and Setup of ESI tool
	2. Provide support to XYZ for setup and utilization of a staging database to prepare flat file data for integration:
	a. Downstream integration of Policy, Plan, Compensation, Account and Contact information from SFDC to SOLAR staging tables.
	b. Upstream integration of Licensed Producer Data from SOLAR to SFDC.
	3. Configure initial integration jobs within ESI from Stored Procedures in the staging database
	4. Educate XYZ on use and maintenance of the ESI tool.

XYZ Responsibilities	1. Provide on-site access for installation of ESI on appropriate hardware.
	2. Freeze feature requests at the beginning of each sprint. Move any additional or changed features realized while a sprint is in progress to the Product Backlog.
	3. Provide remote access during the implementation period for ongoing setup, testing, and support.
	4. Set up the staging database to hold Policy, Plan, Compensation, Account and Contact information from SFDC.
	5. Implement the process to import Salesforce data to a staging database prior to pushing data to the Sold Case system.
	6. Provide details of reporting needs on integrated data (log files, email alerts of success or errant integration job sessions).
	7. Provide both business and technical resources that can sufficiently communicate functional and technical requirements of the required integration.
Evaluation	Analysis of success (roughly 4 weeks after rollout).

Evaluation

The Success Plan should be reviewed on or about 4 weeks after the training date.

Effective Date

The Effective Date of this Success Plan shall be the date that signed approval is given below. The terms of this Success Guarantee and those in the SOW shall expire on MONTH DAY YEAR if XYZ has failed to agree and sign by that date.

This Success Plan must be completed within 4 weeks of the first delivery of the plan to XYZ. Failure by XYZ to approve this Success Plan or comply with the Responsibilities set forth herein will void the terms of the Success Guarantee.

Success Plan Approval

The signatures below certify that both parties agree to the Success Plan as set forth in this document. Bluewolf shall not be held accountable and payment shall not be withheld for criterion not documented in this Success Plan or as a result of a failure by XYZ to meet their obligations for any success criteria identified above.

XYZ   *Bluewolf Group, LLC.*

_____   _____
Authorized Signature   **Authorized Signature**

_____   _____
Name   **Name**

_____   _____
Title   **Title**

_____   _____
Date   **Date**

Printed in the United States
125396LV00005B/1-159/P